What Is True Love?

What Is
True Love?

Jennie McPherson

XULON PRESS

Xulon Press
2301 Lucien Way #415
Maitland, FL 32751
407.339.4217
www.xulonpress.com

© 2021 by Jennie McPherson

All rights reserved solely by the author. The author guarantees all contents are original and do not infringe upon the legal rights of any other person or work. No part of this book may be reproduced in any form without the permission of the author.

Due to the changing nature of the Internet, if there are any web addresses, links, or URLs included in this manuscript, these may have been altered and may no longer be accessible. The views and opinions shared in this book belong solely to the author and do not necessarily reflect those of the publisher. The publisher therefore disclaims responsibility for the views or opinions expressed within the work.

Unless otherwise indicated, Scripture quotations taken from the King James Version (KJV) – *public domain*.

Scripture quotations taken from the Holy Bible, New International Version (NIV). Copyright © 1973, 1978, 1984, 2011 by Biblica, Inc.™. Used by permission. All rights reserved.

Paperback ISBN-13: 978-1-66282-027-4
Ebook ISBN-13: 978-1-66282-312-1

Table of Contents

Chapter 1: What Is True Love?...............1

Chapter 2: Love in Marriage 7

Chapter 3: The Wrong Type of Love 11

Chapter 4: The Right One 15

Chapter 1

WHAT IS TRUE LOVE?

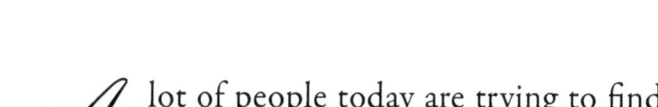

A lot of people today are trying to find true love. But what is it, really?

Some say, "If you don't spend all your time and money on me, then you don't love me." Others think, "If you don't beat me and abuse me, then you don't love me." Even still, others express, "If you don't do what I say or when I say it, then you don't love me."

All these desires are merely demands, not love. In today's world, so many people have different ideas about what love truly is. However, in John 3:16, Jesus clearly explains true love: "For God so loved the world that he gave his only begotten son that whosoever believeth in him should not perish but have everlasting life (KJV)." You see, this is true love, the ultimate love, unconditional love. This is the type of love no man or woman could ever offer. For a Father to give His one and only Son to die on a cross so that the world would be saved…that's love.

Romans 5:8 tells us, "But God commendeth his love toward us, in that while we were yet sinners Christ died for us (KJV)." On the cross, Christ took all our sins upon Himself and died so that we might live. So you see, we should have the same love for others as Christ has for us. John 15:13 says, "Greater love hath no man than this, that a man lay down his life for his friends (KJV)." Furthermore, 1 John 3:16 explains, "Hereby perceive we the love of God because he laid down his life for us and we ought to lay down our lives for the brethren (KJV)." These verses tell us we should be Christlike and love as He does. Regardless of what a person may do or say, we must still show love. For example, when my mom passed away. My dad got a girlfriend and started staying in the family home before my mom was even put in the grave it was hard. Through God all I could do is show love I couldn't treat my dad or even his lady friend wrong. Church people would ask me how can you be nice and smile, help them the way they treated your mom. I would have blown up and gotten mad people would tell me. My response was what kind of Christian would I be if I wouldn't show them love they are lost souls. We can't treat others wrong we have to allow the love of God to shine in our life so that others can see him in our life and repent.

Growing up, true love wasn't in my house at all. Even in my marriage, what I thought was love in reality wasn't. By this time, I had never seen true love between a man and a woman. When I gave my life to God, He began to show me the love I had always wanted to see and know, but not only that—I wanted to feel that love. I can't really explain it—all I know is that this love from God felt good.

Sad to say, but when I had my own children, I couldn't show them love because at that time, I still really didn't know what it was myself. I didn't want to hug my children or even tell them, "I love you." As a parent, I was an example of the fact that it seems we as humans have more time for others than we do for our own families. As I got older and began to grow closer to God, I developed that personal relationship with Him. I knew then I had been so wrong—how I'd missed out on so much with my own children because of my loveless childhood; it wasn't fair to them at all. But the good news is that it's never too late to show my children this love that I have learned about, no matter how old they get. God is still showing me this love and working on me. What I mean is, I'm not the same person I once was. I had a black, sinful heart with a lot of hate. I wanted people to just die, so mean. But now I'm more humble, more loving, and more caring since God has changed my heart. When I see my enemy or a loved one in pain, I'll ask God to place it upon me and not the individual. You see, my God has changed me in more ways than one, and He can do the same for anyone. All I want to do is love people, but with some, that is so hard because when people get their heart broken, it's hard to open up again to anyone. If you allow God to come into your heart, He can change you in a way that only He can. First John 3:16 (KJV) will explain it all for me, "Hereby perceive we the love of God, because he laid down his life for us: and we ought to lay down our lives for the brethren." What this is saying is we should be as Christ. He laid down His life for us—we should have that type of love to do the same for each other.

I am so glad God has no respect of person. Romans 2:11 tells us, "For God does not show favoritism (NIV)." You see, our God is so big that He can show each of us all His love at the same time. Just take a moment to walk outside and feel the wind kiss you upon your face. As the sun shines down on top of you, God is showing you His beautiful glory. When the birds sing in the early morning, they are singing glory to God. If you look at the tops of the pine trees two weeks before Easter, you will see the yellow shoots. The closer it gets to Easter Sunday, the tallest shoot will branch off and form a cross. Most of the pine trees will have small yellow crosses on all the tallest shoots. Easter will be the only time you will be able to see the crosses. Wow...how beautiful. If the trees and animals can praise God, then what is our problem with doing the same? Why can't we be free?

Let go and let God have His way in your life. Without love, we hold one another back; we tie the hands of God so much. And all He wants to do is just love us, but we can't forgive or even love ourselves. That's why we have to allow God, through the Holy Spirit, to work within our hearts. Why can't Christians be like kids today and forgive others who do us wrong?

Chapter 2

LOVE IN MARRIAGE

Many will argue that it takes two to make a marriage, but I've learned from my pastor that it takes three—the husband, the wife, and God in the center. See, we can never leave Christ out of anything in our lives. If we do, then nothing will work out right.

As long as you keep God first in your marriage, everything will work out for the best because God will be leading you and your spouse. Matthew 6:33: "But seek ye first the kingdom of God, and his righteousness and all these things shall be added unto you (KJV)." You could never outdo God.

I've never seen the love between a husband and wife like I did in my own marriage, but it wasn't always like that. It would take about ten years before I would get to see what this love was all about.

During our marriage, I became so sick that I was close to death, and my husband wouldn't leave my side. I had a fever of 104.6 and rising, and doctors couldn't get a blood pressure reading. My potassium was so low; I was freezing cold, hallucinating, and experiencing dehydration. But you know, I would tell my husband, "Go, I'll be fine. I'm just going to rest," but he wouldn't leave. I was so weak that I couldn't stand, more or less walk, so he had to help me to the bathroom. All I wanted was my husband by my side. If I could only touch his skin, I would feel better. If he would walk outside, he would call or text me, saying, "Are you okay? Do you need anything?" He would take care of me like a little child, washing, dressing, and feeding me.

When your spouse takes care of you like that, it's true love, but it took the love of Christ between the both of us to be able to treat one another in such a way. Colossians 3:14 says, "And over all these virtues put on love, which binds them all together in perfect unity (NIV)." God is the one who binds the man and woman together as one.

Genesis 2:24 tells us, "Therefore a man shall leave his father and mother and hold fast to his wife and they shall become one flesh (KJV)." See, this is what my husband did for me. When I got sick, it wasn't up to my parents to take care of me. As husband and wife, it is our job to take care of one another because we are as one now, no longer two. My husband wouldn't even leave and go to work for he was so afraid to leave me, not knowing what would happen to me. During that time, I fell deeply in love with him all over again like never before because I saw how much love this man had for me. Lord, what did I do to deserve this kind of love? I'm nobody special, but through Christ, we are all special.

People say I'm crazy for what I'm about to say, but my prayer is for God to take me home before He takes my husband. I do not want to be here on this earth without the love of my life, my soulmate, my true love. God has given me a love for this man more than words can say. Not many people can say that about their spouse. However, in order for this type of love to grow in a marriage, God must be in the center of it.

Chapter 3

THE WRONG TYPE OF LOVE

In Isaiah 5:20, the Bible says, "Woe to those who call evil good and good evil who put darkness for light and light for darkness who put bitter for sweet and sweet for bitter (KJV)." The word "woe" means great sorrow or distress, trouble, or misery, and who wants that in their life? You see, today, the people of the world think good is bad and bad is good—it's backwards. In His Word, God told us this was going happen before the world began. The way a lot of us were raised, we didn't see a lot of love at home. All we were taught was to work, work, work, but where was the family time or the hugs and kisses from Mom and Dad?

These are just some of the wrong attributes in a marriage that reveal a lack of the real kind of love:

- Keeping God out of the marriage.
- The inability to love one's spouse because one can't love oneself.
- Cheating on one's spouse.
- Beating one's spouse.
- No communication or listening.
- Breaking of one's marriage vows.
- No respect in the marriage.
- The act of trying to fill a hole in one's heart.
- No protection from the husband; the wife will protect her husband more than he will protect her.
- Most of all, a husband and wife's inability or lack of desire to pray for one another.

A marriage with these attributes doesn't have love in it at all. It's a fairy tale full of hoping and wishing for something that's not there. But this is what the world will call right. Who wants to live in a lie the rest of their lives while they are dying on the inside with a broken heart? If this marriage I described sounds like your relationship, allow God to heal your heart. Stop looking for love in the wrong places for men cannot and will not give you what God can. When you have a relationship like this, it brings depression, low self-esteem, hatred in your heart, sickness, and stress. You don't care, and you close your heart up, and doing this is very harmful, not only to yourself but to others also. When you close everyone out of your life, you won't care about hurting anyone's feelings and won't have any compassion. Then people wonder why no one cares or loves them. But you see, the truth about love is if you don't know who Christ is then you don't know what love really is. It will affect others because sometimes people may feel as though they did something to you, but in reality, they didn't. However, when people feel like this, it breaks their hearts because they love you for who you are but you won't allow them into your life. Is this the type of life you want with no one to love? If it is, then continue to keep God out of your relationship with your spouse. However, this causes people to kill themselves or even one another. For example, when there is no communication in a marriage but you see your spouse out talking and laughing with the opposite sex, it forms jealously in the heart, and that's a doorway open for Satan to bring his demons into your marriage to cause even bigger problems. Then you will argue even more on a daily routine about nothing at all. With some marriages, if they can't have you then they don't want anyone else with you either. That's where it becomes dangerous because those people will kill you before they see you with another person. This is why it's very important to put God first.

Chapter 4

THE RIGHT ONE

How do you know the person you have your eyes on is the right one? Easy! Ask God because He knows the future, and He knows each and every one of us inside and out. For instance, the Bible tells us in Matthew 10:30, "But the very hairs of your head are all numbered (KJV)." We don't even know the amount of hairs on our own heads, but God does. That's amazing.

Jeremiah 1:5 (KJV) begins by saying, "Before I formed thee in the belly I knew you..." This means God knew us before we were even thought of. Isaiah 44:24 also tells us, "Thus saith the Lord, thy redeemer and he that formed thee from the womb, I am the Lord that maketh all things: that stretcheth forth the heavens alone: that spreadeth abroad the earth by myself (KJV)."

If God has done all this, then who else besides God would we ask, "Is this the right person for me to marry?" A lot of us might go on about how we feel in the physical side, the human side of us. But if we fail to listen to the Holy Spirit, we make a mess out of our lives and then often end up putting children in the middle of it. When it gets bad, that's when we must look for God to fix. Although, had we from the beginning allowed God in the driver's seat, we would have avoided the mess in the first place. By leaving God out of your marriage, you're asking for trouble, a broken heart, and lots of regret throughout your life. We should allow God to place us with the people we are to marry so we will have peace, joy, happiness, communication, and—most of all—*love.*

Book Summary / Bio

In my book What Is True Love, author Jennie McPherson discusses the different types of love we as humans go through and what to look for in a relationship. I myself have been married twice. My husband and I have five children and getting ready to have our sixth grandchild. We live in North Carolina and have a trucking business. I also do private care, helping the elderly. We are very blessed, God has been good to us this is how I can speak on What Is True Love because of the love of Christ.

www.ingramcontent.com/pod-product-compliance
Lightning Source LLC
LaVergne TN
LVHW021751060526
838200LV00052B/3576

DEDICATION
Thank you to all my readers without you I couldn't do what I love.

INTRODUCTION

Whilst a lot of psychology students and professionals know that anxiety disorders cause people a lot of fear, anxiety and a number of rather extreme physical reactions, a lot of people don't know how Cognitive Behavioural Therapy is used to treat this range of mental health conditions.

No one really breaks Cognitive Behavioural Therapy into its elements and components that make it able to treat anxiety disorders, so I'm hoping to change that slightly with this book.

<u>What Will This Book Cover?</u>

This book will cover a lot of great, brilliant topics with a passionate tone. The book starts off by looking at a number of anxiety disorders and anxiety-related disorders (a very important difference you'll learn about more in the book). Like Social Anxiety Disorder, Generalised Anxiety Disorder, Specific Phobias and more.

All before moving onto the brilliant topics of

Cognitive Behavioural Therapy in the second section, from the cognitive and behavioural theories that underpin this critical therapy to how CBT actually treats these conditions. For example, by using thought records, cognitive interventions and my own personal favourite Behavioural Experiments.

Before we conclude with the great topic of exposure therapy and that was really fun to write about, so I know you'll enjoy reading about it.

Why Buy This Book?

Just like all of my other books, this is a fun brilliant fact-based book that is delivered in an engaging, conversational tone that actually brings the subject material alive. This is NOT a boring, dull book at all and it is packed filled with useful examples that help to demonstrate the theory and how it applies in the real world.

Therefore, if you want an excellent guide to CBT and anxiety disorders delivered in an easy-to-understand and engaging tone that won't make you want to fall asleep then this is definitely the book for you.

Bonus

Also, there's a free bonus essay at the back of the book that explores more about Generalised Anxiety Disorder, how CBT is used to treat it and how Mindfulness-Based Cognitive Therapy is used as well. It's a great essay that will help to deepen your knowledge about this topic even more.

Who Am I?

Personally, I always love to know who the author is of the nonfiction I read so I know the information is coming from a good source. In case you're like me, I'm Connor Whiteley, the internationally bestselling author of over 40 psychology books.

In addition, I am the host of *The Psychology World Podcast,* a weekly show exploring a new psychology topic each week and delivering the latest psychology news. Available on all major podcast apps and YouTube.

Finally, I am a psychology graduate studying a Clinical Psychology Masters at the University of Kent, England.

So now we know more about each other, let's dive into the great topic of anxiety disorders and CBT.

CBT FOR ANXIETY

PART ONE: INTRODUCTION TO ANXIETY DISORDERS

CBT FOR ANXIETY

INTRODUCTION TO ANXIETY DISORDERS

In all honesty, there is little point just talking about Cognitive Behavioural Therapy without introducing and recapping on anxiety disorders first. Since we need to understand or remember these conditions before we can look at how to treat them.

As well as anxiety disorders are critical to understanding anyway, not only because of how common they are but also because there are so many facets, and differences between the different conditions.

Therefore, in this first section of the book we'll be exploring the different types of anxiety disorders along with their "unique" (to some extent) diagnostic criteria and other great pieces of information.

<u>What is Anxiety?</u>

To kick off this section, I think anxiety is certainly one of those words that we know what it means to some extent but none of us know how to exactly define it. Hence, I want to define anxiety up front so we're all on the same page.

Anxiety is in a lot of cases an adaptive response to a real threat or danger. For example, anxiety is great if you go into an old abandoned building that is dangerous because the floors and structure might not be sound. That is a good case of anxiety because going into an old abandoned house could be dangerous.

Another useful case of anxiety is if you meet up with a date for the first time after meeting them on an online dating app. This could be useful because you'll be careful and you know that's small chance that your online date could not be who they say they are.

Additionally, anxiety causes fear, which is the emotional response to a real or perceived imminent threat and the anxiety is caused by this anticipation of a future threat.

Again this is normally a great tool that has aided humans in survival for thousands of years.

Also, it's worth noting that anxiety disorders are moderately common as the lifetime prevalence, how common the condition is in a population, of this condition is 29% (Kessler et al, 2005) and it's more common in women than men. (Bresula, Chilcoal, Kessler and Davis, 1999)

What Are Anxiety Disorders?

Nonetheless, this anxiety turns into a mental health difficulty when this goes to excessive levels and causing a person to experience excessive anxiety and fear, disturb their behaviour and feel an out-of-proportion sense of danger.

Which results in significant distress and it interferences with a people's core areas of functioning. For example, a person might not be able to hold down a job because they're always late as they're checking things and other examples we will look at through the first section of the book.

Now on a minor aside note, I want to mention why I don't call excessive levels of anxiety a mental health *problem*. This is simply a language choice because the term "problem" sounds like we are blaming our client, like their anxiety is their fault, it's their problem and why should we have to deal with their them being messed up. That is what the term "problem" sounds like to me and the vast majority of clinical psychologists so I wanted to clean that up.

And another factor that really helps to distinguish "normal" anxiety and clinical anxiety, if you will, is that disturbance of behaviour, distress and everyday functioning. We are all anxious about different things but we can all largely function and get on with our lives.

People with anxiety conditions cannot do such things.

Furthermore, the most common anxiety disorders in no particular order are:
- Social Anxiety Disorder (also known as Social Phobia)
- Panic Disorder

- Specific Phobia
- Agoraphobia
- Separation Anxiety Disorder
- Generalised Anxiety Disorder

I'm sure some of you are wondering why there are a bunch of other conditions that should be there but aren't. For example, PTSD, OCD amongst a few others and this is because these are no longer classed as Anxiety Disorders.

Instead these are classed informally as Anxiety-Related Disorders and formally Trauma and Stressor-related Disorders. Including mental health conditions like, obsessive-compulsive disorder (OCD) and post-traumatic stress disorder (PTSD)

What Makes Up An Anxiety Disorder?

Whilst there a number of unique facets of each type of disorder, to wrap up this introductory chapter, I wanted to mention that all anxiety disorders occur because people believe that certain situations are more dangerous than they actually are and they're made up of four components.

There's a cognitive component relating to a person's unrealistic thoughts about their fear of loss of control and how they exaggerate the danger. Then there is an emotional component too that focuses on how the disorder causes a person's terror, irritability and panic.

Furthermore, an anxiety disorder has a physical component that is responsible for a person's activation of their hormonal system and sympathetic nervous system resulting in their flight-or-fight response to be activated. This is also the same component causing heart palliations and sweating. As well as there's the behavioural factor of the disorder that causes an anxious person to change their behaviour like developing maladaptive coping mechanisms, like avoiding the source of their anxiety.

We'll look at all of this in more depth in the next few chapters but this is all important to really understand the effects of anxiety on a person and then how do we treat them with CBT later on.

WHAT IS PANIC DISORDER AND SOCIAL ANXIETY DISORDER?

Whilst the entire purpose of this first section is to help you recap and understand what different anxiety disorders are, I want to personally promise you that this is interesting. It's certainly more interesting than I originally thought because we look at the different conditions themselves, their diagnostic criteria which is critical because of a number of points I make, and we need to understand this stuff so we can understand why CBT works for anxiety.

What Is Panic Disorder And Agoraphobia?

Personally, I always think that panic disorders are one of the worst anxiety disorders because this is a type of anxiety disorder that can be characterised by a person having repeated or debilitating panic attacks. With these attacks being a sudden episode of horrific bodily symptoms. Like: choking, chest pains and distress.

As well as whilst all anxiety disorders do involve

panic attacks to various extents and normally a panic attack in any other disorder is limited to only the anxious stimuli like a social situation or spiders, but a panic disorder involves panic attacks that come out the blue.

For instance, whilst I once knew a girl that suffered from Social Anxiety Disorder so she had panic attacks in social situations, it was only those situations. Where a person with Panic Disorder would suffer from a panic attack in any situation. As well as panic disorders are found in 5% of women and 2% of men. (Barlow, 2002).

As a result, when it comes to understanding panic disorders, we need to look at the following three types:

- Panic disorder without agoraphobia
- Panic disorder with agoraphobia
- Agoraphobia without a history of panic disorder

Also, agoraphobia without panic disorders are the same as the above but this condition is focused on panic-like symptoms and not full-blown panic attacks.

<u>What Is Agoraphobia?</u>

Personally, I feel that agoraphobia isn't a very well-used word and it really isn't known about so agoraphobia is a form of anxiety coming from a person being in situations where escape is embarrassing or difficult or help isn't perceived to be available in the event of a panic or panic-like symptoms. For example, agoraphobia can be found in situations when a person is far from home because the person might not know who to turn to for help, and the same goes for travel and crowds.

Consequently, the person with agoraphobia will avoid these situations or if they go into these situations this will produce a lot of anxiety or they will need a companion to enter these situations. This helps with the issues surrounding the situation being difficult to escape and helping not being available. As well as if a person does want a diagnosis of agoraphobia then this condition needs to be able to explain the person's symptoms better than another disorder.

What Would A Panic Attack and Panic Disorder Diagnosis Require?

When it comes to getting a diagnosis, we all know that a set list of criteria has to be met in the Diagnostic and Statistical Manual Version 5 (DSM-5) for a diagnosis to be made, so all this information is from the DSM-5 (APA, 2013).

Therefore, for a person to meet Criterion A for Panic Disorders (and as this is the Criterion that gives you the best idea about the feelings a Panic Disorder gives a person, this is the only one we'll look at), a person must experience an abrupt surge from a calm or anxious state to one of intense discomfort or fear that peaks within minutes and during this time four or more of the following symptoms must happen:

- Sweat

- Tremble
- Shake
- Have a feeling of choking
- Experience palpitation, accelerated heart rate or pounding heart
- Experience chest pains or discomfort
- Feel dizzy, unsteady, faint or light-headed
- Have a fear of dying
- Experience a sense of smothering or shortness of breath
- Have a sense of numbness or tingling
- Nausea or abdominal distress
- Chills or heat sensations
- Fear losing control or "going crazy"
- Experience a feeling of unreality (Derealisation) or being detached from themselves (depersonalisation)

This is why I rather like looking at the diagnostic criteria for different mental health conditions, because they help to give a real sense about what it is like to experience these conditions, and then using this knowledge we can start to think about possible ways to treat these symptoms.

Social Anxiety Disorder (APA, 2013)

This definitely has to be the most famous anxiety condition so whilst I probably don't have to introduce it too much, I still really want to. As a result of social anxiety disorder is defined as high levels of fear or anxiety about one or more social situations where the person is exposed to scrutiny by others.

This fear and anxiety are caused by the person's fear that they will act in a way or show their anxiety symptoms that will lead to the other people negatively evaluating them. In other words, negatively judging them so the person will be humiliated, embarrassed and rejected by the other people.

Also when I was first learning this topic, I found it rather surprising that social anxiety disorder isn't one thing. Since a person could be fine at parties but have social anxiety disorder when talking in public, talking in a classroom or not at all. The entire point of social anxiety disorder is that a person's anxiety and fear could be provoked by a single type of social situation, most or all social situations. It really does depend on the person.

Furthermore, men and women are affected equally by this disorder as well as it typically manifests itself in childhood or adolescence (Robins and Regier, 1991).

A Social Anxiety Disorder Diagnosis

When it comes to a person wanting a diagnosis, there is a set list of symptoms and behaviours they have to meet. For instance, for a person to have social anxiety disorder they need to experience a high level of fear or anxiety about one or more social situations where the person is exposed to possible scrutiny by other people.

For example, the DSM-5 includes examples like social interactions, like meeting unfamiliar people and having a conversation, performing in front of others, like doing public speaking, and being observed, like eating or drinking.

In addition, the anxiety or fear they experience has to be out of proportion to the real threat posed by the social situation and the sociocultural context. This is an idea we'll return to in the Specific Phobia chapter.

Moreover, the social situation must almost always provoke a fear or anxiety reaction in a person, as well as the person must show that they avoid these situations or when they are exposed to these situations, the person has to endure them with intense anxiety or fear.

And then because the DSM-5 loves a good old time factor (a very common theme throughout the book), the person has to have a persistent fear, anxiety or avoidance of these situations for at least 6 months or more. As well as (by the end of this first section you'll be saying this with me) the fear, anxiety, or avoidance of social situations must cause clinically significant distress or impairment for the person in social, occupational, or other important areas of functioning.

So now we understand how Panic Disorders and Social Anxiety works, what is PTSD?

WHAT IS PTSD?

Moving onto the most potentially well-known anxiety-related disorder, Post-Traumatic Stress Disorder (PTSD) is a condition that has thankfully received a lot of media and fictional interest over the years. And whilst I don't normally say this, I think in the case of PTSD this has been a good thing.

Especially as since it relates to soldiers and the US in my experience show a zealous devotion to their servicemen and women, this devotion has basically been infused into the films and TV programmes, so compared to other conditions (like psychosis, depression and schizophrenia), PTSD is presented relatively truthfully and this really has helped people to have a good sense of what PTSD is.

Therefore, because PTSD involves intrusive thoughts and memories, this experience is very anxiety-provoking to people with the condition so this is why we need to look at it in this book. As well as whilst there is evidence that PTSD is also a healing mechanism as the mind is trying to make a person confront their past for lack of a better term, this is important to realise but it is still a very anxiety-provoking experience.

As a result, for a person to get a diagnosis of PTSD, they have to meet Criterion A, meaning they have to have one of the following. A person has to be exposed to death, the threat of death, actual or threatened sexual violence, actual or threatened serious injury in one of the following ways:

- They need to directly experience the event or events themselves
- They have to witness these events happening to other people in person, so this cannot be witnessed online.
- They need to have been repeatedly exposed or have extreme exposure to aversive details of traumatic events.

And that last one is flat out critical in how professionals get PTSD, because if you're a police officer, mental health worker or someone working with child sexual abuse victims then having to hear about the worse of humanity every single day of your working life will have some sort of effect on you. This is why some professionals develop PTSD without having experienced the trauma themselves.

In addition, a client would have to present one or more of these intrusive symptoms to be diagnosed with PTSD, as well as it's good to note that these intrusive symptoms *have* to be associated with the traumatic event. This is to eliminate these symptoms being caused by another mental health condition.

- Repeatedly having distressing dreams about the event
- Repeatedly having intrusive, involuntary memories associated with the event
- Experiencing dissociative reactions, like flashbacks, that make the person feel or react just like the event was happening.

For example, a soldier might react like they were actually being fired upon by the enemy even when they're walking into a supermarket.

- They would have to experience a prolonged period or intense psychological distress after being exposed to internal or external cues that symbolise or remind them of an aspect of the traumatic event.

This is why certain loud noises that sort of resemble gunshots can be very triggering to soldiers.

- Having clear physiological reactions to these cues.

Moreover, for Criterion C, a person could need to show they persistently avoid stimuli associated with the traumatic event by showing or proving evidence by avoiding or taking effort to avoid the distressing memories, feelings or thoughts associated with the trauma and/ or they would be able to prove the avoid or take efforts to avoid external reminders that trigger these distressing memories, thoughts or feelings of the trauma.

For instance, you might find PTSD sufferers don't go outside to crowded places because the crowds remind them of the crowded streets of Afghanistan were a suicide bomber struck, for example.

Moreover, when it comes to Criterion D of PTSD, people need to experience negative changes in their mental processes and mood in relation to the trauma, by having two of the following:

- An inability to recall an important aspect of the trauma (also known as them blocking it out of their mind)
- Having exaggerated and persistent negative beliefs about themselves, others and the world.

Anyone familiar with Major Depression Disorder may have heard that before because it is the Cognitive Triad, and this why you need to rule out other mental health conditions (as mentioned later) since a person could be depressed or have PTSD. This is why a person needs to have all of these criterions.

- A noticeable and potentially dramatic decreased in interest or taking part in activities.

Sounds similar to depression, doesn't it?

- Have feelings of estrangement or detachment from others
- Have persistent problems experiencing positive emotions

Again, it sounds like depression.

- Persistently have distorted mental processes about the causes and/ or consequences of the traumatic event leading to them blaming themselves or others.
- Be persistently in a negative emotional state like shame, horror, fear or anger.

Penultimately, we know that PTSD causes people to experience massive changes in how they react in situations and their arousal to stimuli. As a result, in the diagnosis process, this needs to be found and this proof is found by a person having any two of the following:

- Showing and doing reckless, self-destructive behaviour
- Showing angry outbursts and irritable behaviour
- Being hypervigilant
- Having problems concentrating
- Experiencing sleep disturbances
- Showing exaggerated startle responses.

Something important to point out here is that the fact that two of those behaviours are needed is critical to understand. Since the whole debate about clinical cut-offs is something for another day, but if a lot of behaviours happened without any of the others then it certainly isn't a big deal at all.

For example, everyone has problems sleeping from time to time, everyone shows exaggerated startle responses sometimes and everyone shows angry outbursts sometimes these all happen for long periods of time. If that happens then it's nothing special but when all these symptoms start happening together and for the same basic length of time, then that's how you know a mental health condition could have developed.

So in case you were ever wondering why the DSM-5 was so strict about people having to have a certain number of symptoms you now know.

Finally, some other criteria that people have to meet is that these disturbances have to last longer than a month, they naturally have to cause clinically significant distress or impairment of their functioning (just like every other condition) as well as the disturbances cannot be attributed to any medical condition or substances.

<u>Acute Stress Disorder</u>

Lastly, for this chapter I wanted to mention Acute Stress Disorder because the diagnostic criteria is similar to PTSD in terms that people need to have experienced criterion A for diagnosis of PTSD to be diagnosed. As well as their symptoms could begin within 3 days to 1 month of the traumatic event and will last for at least 3 days and up to 1 month.

In other words, this is still a persistent and severe mental health condition similar to PTSD but it doesn't last as long.

Also, it's very possible that a person could get diagnosed with Acute Stress Disorder but actually have PTSD because of a misdiagnosis, someone thinking their symptoms only lasted 30 weeks when actually they're still ongoing they just don't recognise the symptoms, or something similar.

WHAT IS GENERALISED ANXIETY DISORDER AND SPECIFIC PHOBIAS?

Whilst I really love Generalised Anxiety Disorder because it is a truly fascinating condition, and you can learn more about the condition itself and how CBT and Mindfulness-Based Cognitive Therapy is used to treat it in the essay at the back of the book, in this chapter I want to introduce you to this great condition.

Now of course, like all mental health conditions, I use the term "great" to help get people interested in the condition so they can learn about it, hopefully become inspired and they might then become specialised or focus in that area, so they can get more people with that condition. I use the term "great" to inspire future or current psychologists into treating that condition, not to minimise the severe impact of any mental health condition.

As a result, Generalised Anxiety Disorder is a very special kind of anxiety disorder because social anxiety is limited to social situations and stimuli, OCD is sort of limited to whatever the obsession or compulsion is and a specific phobia is limited to whatever the specificity is. Like dogs, horses or spiders.

Consequently, if a person doesn't run into any of the anxiety-provoking stimuli then to be honest, they can live a relatively clinically normal life as if you remove the source of their anxiety then they don't get anxious.

That's just an example here, of course the client does need psychotherapy to get rid of their anxiety and they can overcome the previously-anxiety provoking stimuli once more.

However, Generalised Anxiety Disorder sadly doesn't have that "benefit" because people with Generalised Anxiety Disorder become anxious about everything and there is not a single source of their anxiety. This makes it next to impossible to live with and it is even harder to treat because it makes targeting very difficult.

As well as not only do people with Generalised Anxiety Disorder worry about everything and anything, but people with the condition also feel inadequate, they can't concentrate, they're oversensitive and may sometimes suffer from insomnia. With Rickels and Ryan (2001) also mentioning that these behaviours can be accompanied by irregular breathing, chronic diaherria, rapid heart rate and excessive sweating.

On the whole, I think it's fairly safe to say this is unfortunately the worse type of anxiety disorder to have, and thankfully there are treatment options which we will look at later on.

Furthermore, Generalised Anxiety Disorder is relatively common as it has a prevalence rate of 6% (Kessler et al, 2005) as well as it's twice as likely to be found in women than men.

Also, this is a great quote summarising Generalised Anxiety Disorder from White (1999) page 72: "I'm so nervous about making a mistake at work I take all my reports home to rewrite them the night before I'm supposed to hand them in".

What Is The Diagnostic Criteria For Generalised Anxiety Disorder?

For a person to get a diagnosis of Generalised Anxiety Disorder, they have to have an excessive level of anxiety and worry that's occurring more days than not for at least a period of 6 months and this anxiety has to be about a number of events or activities.

In other words, a person cannot *only* be worried about school for the past 6 months or be *only* worried about work. They have to be worried excessively about work, school and maybe other areas of their life and the activities they do.

Additionally, the client would have to find it difficult to control their worry. As well as their anxiety and worry would have to be associated with three or more of the following 6 symptoms in adults or 1 in children (I'll talk more about this in a moment) and these symptoms would have to be present more days than not in the past 6 months.

- Being easily fatigued
- Having muscle tension
- Being irritable
- Having difficulty concentrating or their mind going blank
- Restlessness, feeling on edge or keyed up
- Experiencing sleep disturbance like having a difficulty staying or falling asleep, being restless or having unsatisfying sleep.

Now during one of my lectures, someone actually mentioned why is it three for adults but only one for children. And whilst my lecturer wasn't a 100% sure because in her experience, it was sort of rare for a child to come forward with this condition. She proposed it is because children don't show some of these symptoms, they don't have the vocabulary to describe these or there are other ways that children exhibit generalised anxiety disorder.

As well as if we think about it, I do sort of see where she is coming from because muscle tension is a weird one for children, because how would a child explain that? I'm an adult and I think even I would struggle. I know it's a strain or aching of a muscle but would that be enough of an explanation for someone to understand what it is?

We need to remember that some children (if not most) don't know what muscle tension or restlessness actually is?

That's why language is important to bear in mind in clinical psychology, even more so when it comes to young children.

Penultimately, for a client to get a Generalised Anxiety Disorder diagnosis, they would need to show that the physical, worry and anxiety symptoms cause them clinically significant levels of distress or impairment in social, occupational, or other important areas of functioning.

Finally, we, as future or current psychologists, would need to know these disturbances are flat out not because of the physiological effects of a substance (like illegal drugs) and not better explained by another mental health condition.

<u>Specific Phobia</u>

I fully admit this is a flat out weird name for this anxiety disorder because whenever we talk about phobias we call them, well, phobias or we name it. Yet the actual grouping name for these anxiety disorders is specific phobia and that is what we will investigate next in this chapter.

Therefore, a specific phobia is a persistent and irrational fear of a specific situation or object. Such as they could be a phobia of heights, animals, flying, seeing injections (but come on, no one likes seeing them) and seeing blood. As well as nearly 5% of the population suffers from some kind of mild form of a phobic disorder.

Additionally, the difference between a fear and a phobia is when a person avoids the fear at all costs and causes them to disrupt their lives. For instance, I personally know my mother does not like spiders and it is a basic "fear" but if there's a spider she still goes into a room and does what she needs to do. That is because she has a minor fear of spiders, not a phobia. Whereas a person with a phobia would probably scream, shout and absolutely refuse to go into the room.

In addition, when it comes to the situations and objects of a phobia, these almost always provoke immediate fear or anxiety, and the critical detail that makes phobias a mental health condition is that the fear or anxiety is always out of proportion to the actual danger posed by the specific object or situation and the sociocultural context.

For example, if we go back to my spider example, I live in England for now and we don't have many deadly spiders and the chance of us seeing a deadly spider is slim-to-none. Therefore, if someone screams, shouts and avoids going into a room with spiders because they believe they will die. Then this is an overreaction to the real risk, but if the same happened in Africa in an area with well-known deadly spiders, then this is not a phobia most probably.

As a result, the phobic situation or object is avoided at all costs or the person might have to endure it with intense fear and anxiety, and then it is that living with intense fear and anxiety that creates additional strains on their mental health and well-being.

Finally, for a diagnosis of a specific phobia, the object or situation must cause a person anxiety, fear and/ or avoidance that results in clinically significant impairment in social, occupational, or other important areas of functioning or distress. As well as these negative feelings must persist for at least 6 months or more.

Also I suppose this does raise an interesting question about mental health services because you could ask, are we making people endure these very severe and painful mental health conditions for a long time?

Basically we are putting them through 6 months of emotional pain and fear just to tick a little box.

Personally, I don't think so because this is how we differ different conditions, but that question is worth thinking about especially if you ever read about the sometimes stupid nature of clinical cut-offs. And how it is in the public service's best interests to filter out some of the people who need help.

Anyway, that is just interesting food for thought.

WHAT IS OBSESSIVE-COMPULSIVE DISORDER?

To wrap up this first section of the book, Obsessive-Compulsive Disorder is certainly a disorder we have to look at because, even though it is no longer classed as an anxiety disorder in the DSM-5, it is still synonymous in the minds of many people with anxiety.

<u>What Is Obsessive-Compulsive Disorder?</u>

Therefore, according to the DSM-5 (APA, 2013), we need to break down this disorder into its two main components. The obsession and the compulsion as with this disorder you cannot have one without the other and each of them is its own aspect.

For example, an obsession is a persistent as well as recurring thought, image or urge that a person experiences and this is unwanted, intrusive and disturbing and in many people this is caused by high levels of anxiety or distress.

Then normally in these cases, a person would

attempt to suppress or ignore these thoughts, images or urges or they're trying to neutralise them by some method, like actually doing the compulsion.

For example, the most common obsession, at least favoured by Hollywood and TV programmes, is dirt. This is why a lot of people who have a cleanliness or dirt obsession are constantly cleaning because they want to neutralise their urge to make sure their house is tidy and spotless.

However, a compulsion is very different because these are repetitive behaviours, like checking the order of something or hand washing, or they're mental acts, like repeating words and counting silently.

People do this because they feel driven to perform these mental actions or behaviours in response to an obsession or according to some rule that must be rigidly applied. Therefore, these behaviours and acts are aimed at reducing and preventing psychological distress for the client or to prevent some dreaded situation or event.

And yet in reality, these acts and behaviours aren't connected in any realistic way to what they're designed to prevent or neutralise or are clearly excessive.

For example, if you have a cleanliness obsession then it *might* be wise to wipe the sides of your kitchen or your coffee table. The things that people and you are going to see the most, but deep cleaning your *entire* house. That isn't logical and that is very excessive and there lies the line between what's clinically normal and what's clinically "abnormal".

Additionally, these obsessions and compulsions are time consuming, like they disturb and take more than an hour a day, and they cause clinically significant distress or an impairment in a person's social, occupational, and other important areas of functioning.

As well as this is what's important to bear in mind when it comes to clinical psychology, something is only really a mental health condition or difficulty when it comes to psychological distress and disturbs people's lives and that is why OCD is important to treat, because these obsessions and compulsions do negatively impact lives, and it can even ruin them.

And that is why current or future clinical psychologists are just so critical so we can improve lives, help people and decrease their psychological distress.

That's exactly where the next section of the book comes in.

PART TWO: COGNITIVE BEHAVIOURAL THERAPY FOR ANXIETY DISORDERS

INTRODUCTION TO COGNITIVE BEHAVIOURAL THERAPY

Now that we're getting onto the part of the book we've all been waiting for, let's start learning about the amazing topic of Cognitive Behavioural Therapy.

As a result, we first need to know both the cognitive and behavioural theories that Cognitive Behavioural Therapy is built on before we can ever hope to understand how CBT works for anxiety disorders.

Therefore, as you can probably imagine Cognitive Behavioural Therapy is based (at least in part) on the cognitive approach to behaviour. As well as Westbrook, Kennerley & Kirk (2007) noted that there is evidence that a lot of mental health conditions are associated with a wide range of cognitive factors. For example, many conditions cause people to have information processing biases, faulty belief schemas as well as dysfunctional ways of thinking.

Then if we apply this logic to anxiety disorders then we've already discussed in the book how anxiety causes a person to have faulty belief systems about how dangerous the stimuli is, the dysfunctional ways they develop to "cope" with the anxiety and their bias information processing because how they perceive the stimuli.

Also, the cognitive approaches to treatment were first pioneered by Albert Ellis (1962) and Aaron Beck (1967) with their aim being to incorporate cognitive processes into psychology, all whilst still maintaining an empirical approach to this because they wanted to avoid ungrounded speculation.

In other words, they wanted to make sure their findings withstood empirical scrutiny and it is a brilliant thing that they set out with this in mind.

In addition, when it comes to cognitive approaches, this view focuses on the idea that a mental health condition is caused by a person developing irrational beliefs, dysfunctional ways of thinking and biased information processing like we saw earlier. And this leads to the person's mental processes being impacted heavily.

For instance, the way a person behaves and emotionally reacts to a stimuli is strongly influenced by their cognition. Like their beliefs, thoughts and interpretation. As well as this impacts how a person reacts to an event too.

For example, because I personally don't find spiders anxiety-provoking, if I see a spider then I don't interpret this as dangerous, life-threatening and I'm not overwhelmed by the emotion of fear. Yet if an anxious person saw a spider then their cognitive processes would tell them this is a life-threatening situation and they will react completely differently to me because the anxious person has biased cognitive processes.

Furthermore, the cognitive approach believes mental health conditions develop and the mental health difficulties onset because of cognitive factors (obviously) but both functional and dysfunctional beliefs develop earlier on, and these beliefs may not cause difficulties for a long period of time.

And this is something that I personally find very interesting about mental health. A person could have depression, ADHD, autism or another condition and function absolutely perfectly. They can hold down a job, have tons of friends (if they want) and live a perfectly happy life, but it is only when they start to struggle and need help is when clinical psychology is really needed.

And something that I personally love to remind people is that a mental health condition isn't a death sentence like some people sadly believe it is. Sure a person with a mental health condition might need a little more support, guidance and treatment but given all of those things there is a good chance they could live a very happy and relatively clinically "normal" life.

Nonetheless, if the person does experience a critical incident event, also known as encounters the anxiety-provoking stimuli, then this would be a disturbing event to them, this could activate their negative beliefs and then lead to a distressing emotional response.

What's The Cognitive-Behavioural Approach?

Building on both the cognitive approaches, to form Cognitive Behavioural Therapy, this approach has to be combined with behavioural approaches. Therefore, whilst the cognitive approach focuses on a person's cognitions and beliefs and how these might lead to particular behaviours. It is these behaviours that are actually a core factor in maintaining or changing beliefs and emotions. Meaning this can become a very vicious cycle.

In other words, a person's negative cognition and beliefs cause negative behaviours. Then these behaviours reinforce the cognitions and beliefs and so on. Since it's the behaviour in a person's response to a negative experience or cognition that could have a significant effect on whether the emotion persists.

For example, if a person reacts badly to a spider then of course the person will want to avoid spiders to avoid this feeling again. Hence, they develop avoidance behaviours. Like, avoiding the situation and event completely, escaping it or engaging in safety behaviours.

Now personally, I love safety behaviours and I think they are truly fascinating because to be honest they have to be some of the biggest cons in psychology. Due to safety behaviours are fully intended to protect us from threat or prevent harm coming to us. As a result, these safety behaviours might reduce our anxiety in the short term, but they always have the unintended consequence of maintaining anxiety in the longer term.

That's why I think safety behaviours are very interesting cons that we pull on ourselves because we convince ourselves that we're helping ourselves to be less anxious, and if we don't do these behaviours we're going to basically die. But in reality, they're making us "worse", not "better.

Core Treatment Components

When it comes to what CBT actually involves, there are a few flat out critical elements that make up this amazingly effective and fascinating therapy.

Firstly, there is a lot of cognitive restructuring involved. This component involves challenging and modifying a person's negative thoughts as well as their dysfunctional beliefs. This is typically done by examining the evidence for a person's beliefs.

For example, we'll talk a lot more about cognitive intervention in two chapters' time but an anxious person will believe their safety behaviours save them and without their safety behaviours they will basically die. That is how powerful these behaviours are, so as you'll see in two chapters a therapist can challenge these beliefs by using experiments and testing whether or not there is evidence to support these beliefs.

Another core feature of CBT is it involves a

therapist helping to modify a person's tendency to indulge in unhelpful thinking processes, this relates to the cognitive biases we spoke about earlier, so the therapist works with the client to modify and reduce these unhelpful mental processes. Like, how a person pays excessive attention to the threat, how they ruminate on the anxiety provoking stimuli and they engage in mental checking.

As well as when it comes to helping a person reduce their unhelpful behaviours, this includes things like reducing their avoidance, safety and checking behaviours. Also CBT involves behavioural experiments (definitely more on that later) and exposure and response prevention (again more on that in a later chapter).

Levels Of Cognition

Of course, we could never ever hope to learn about cognitive approaches and CBT without looking at levels of cognition, and this is absolutely critical when it comes to Cognitive Behavioural Therapy. Since a person's levels of cognition are as follows:

- Their automatic thoughts
- Their intermediate beliefs, attitudes and rules which are assumptions about the world and the self.
- Their core beliefs. Their basic beliefs about their self, others and the world.

And this idea about levels of cognition is flat out critical in CBT because a therapist has to be very careful when they do cognitive restructuring because you cannot hope to change someone's core beliefs automatically. That just isn't how things work but you can start off with challenging and modifying a person's automatic thoughts then their intermediate beliefs and then their core beliefs.

You need to work "slowly" and gradually for the therapy to work.

An anxiety example of how a therapist might go about finding out what a person's core belief is, is as follows:

- I'm terrified of spiders (automatic thought)
- I know if a spider gets near me it could attack me (potential intermediate belief)
- If a spider touches me then I know for a fact I'm going to get bitten and I'll be rushed to hospital (potential core belief)

Now I have to admit that it is far, far easier to come up with potential levels of cognitions with depression for teaching purposes but you get the general idea. A CBT therapist would have to effectively peel back the layers of a person's cognition to truly understand why they have these biased mental processes.

Thinking Errors/Biases

If you've studied depression then you might be familiar with this section of the chapter because there are a lot of commonalities between all types of CBT (at least "first-wave" therapies) and the types of cognitive biases and errors a CBT therapist would encounter. Therefore, here are the following cognitive errors a therapist is likely to encounter and I have broken them up so you can clearly see the error and an example of what it is like:

- All or nothing- if I can't love all dogs then I'm scared of all of them.
- Exaggerated standards/expectations- if I can't pet a dog then I'm a failure (a potential example at least)
- Catastrophising- my life is over because if I go outside I might see a dog and it might kill me.

- Selective attention to the negative/threat- a person is basically always drawn to anxiety provoking stimuli.
- Over-generalising- "I'm scared of my brother's pet dog so I'm scared of all dogs"
- Dismissing the positive- I might be able to stroke my sister's dog but I feel worthless and scary around all other dogs. I'm so lame.

- Magnifying/minimising- minimising the positive and magnifying the bad
- Jumping to conclusions
- Emotional reasoning- being irrational and basing your reason on emotion, not fact.
- Personalising
- Internalising/externalising

Again, some of those examples might sound similar to depression and that is to be expected considering there is a comorbidity between depression and anxiety in some people.

Role Of Avoidance And Safety Behaviours

Returning to my topic and building upon what we learnt earlier, a very good definition of a safety behaviour can be found in Salkovskis (1988, 1991):

"A behaviour which is performed in order to prevent or minimise a feared catastrophe"

As well as we know that safety behaviours have several effects on a person's beliefs. Like they prevent a person from getting disconfirming evidence about their beliefs (this is flat out critical for the information in two chapters' time), this can increase the sensation a person experiences like their anxiety and fear, and safety behaviours increase their rumination and preoccupation with the anxiety provoking stimuli.

Overall, all these effects on behaviour that safety behaviours cause are linked together to make the person focus on the stimuli they find threatening and this of course isn't helpful.

Hence, the need for CBT for anxiety disorders which is what we'll look at in a moment after we understand more about the behavioural approach.

BEHAVIOURAL APPROACH

Building upon the last chapter, we need to dive into the Behavioural aspect of CBT a little more since CBT is also built on the idea of Behaviour Therapy as designed by Wolpe (1958).

Now behaviour therapy views mental health difficulties as the result of things we've learnt as reactions to different life experiences, and it looks at learning theory to explain mental health conditions. This was originally seen to be more empirical and objective than the cognitive and other approaches, but personally I'm not so sure. But again I am talking as a person bought up on modern standards, this actually *might* have been better than other approaches in the 50s.

Anyway, behaviour therapy focuses on the belief that dysfunctional behaviours, just like with adaptive behaviours, are acquired through learning and if something can be learnt, it can be unlearnt.

Now, because this can sometimes be as clear as

mud, a potential example would be because a person saw a spider and it "attacked" them. The person learnt to react negatively to all spiders because one spider attacked them. It's a very basic example but it shows the point well.

Additionally, because behaviour therapy is built on learning therapy, there are two core principles that are flat out critical to this therapy.

Firstly, you have classical conditioning saying there is a learnt association between two stimuli, the conditioned stimuli predicts the occurrence of the unconditioned stimuli.

Secondly, you have operant conditioning where a person learns a specific behaviour or response and this behaviour leads to a rewarding or reinforcing behaviour.

As well as before I go onto more of the behaviour therapy stuff, I want to point out that this is an important theory that does in a way unpin a lot of modern CBT. Since part of CBT's job is to help work a person's maintaining factors (what helps a person to maintain and not change their maladaptive behaviours) and the easiest "conditioned" factor for a mental health condition would be when a person has an anxiety attack and for the first time ever their family pays attention to them.

If you're starved of attention and love and your mental health condition seems to be the only thing capable of making people in your life seem interested in you, you are flat out not going to change. That's a maintaining factor and a conditioned response according to this theory.

As a result, going back to behavioural approach topics, people can experience positive reinforcement and this can benefit a mental health condition. Since this is when a behaviour leads to an introduction of a desirable stimuli (like a parent's love or attention). Equally, behavioural theory mentions negative reinforcement as well. This is when the behaviour or response leads to the removal of an aversive stimulus. Overall, both of these types of reinforcement are rewarding so this leads to an increase in how common the behaviour is.

Moreover, as you can imagine when there is a type of punishment, when the behaviour leads to an introduction of aversive stimuli, this leads to a reduction in the frequency of the behaviour but I don't think this really comes up too much in clinical psychology. The last thing we want to do, as future or current psychologists, is actively expose people to unpleasant stimuli.

Overall, psychologists can use this theory to explain how certain disruptive and maladaptive behaviours develop and are maintained because of rewarding or positive outcomes.

Linking This To Anxiety

To wrap up this chapter, I just want to run through explicitly how this all links to anxiety so everyone understands how the behavioural approach to anxiety works. Therefore, according to classical conditioning, which can explain how certain emotional disorders are formed, a person experiences a phobic stimuli (this is the conditioned stimulus) and this leads to them associating this response with the distressing event (this becomes the unconditioned stimulus).

In addition, we can use operant conditioning to understand how behaviours in anxious people could have developed and are maintained. This includes, avoidance behaviours and safety behaviours, as well as any disruptive behaviours that could lead to their attention or them escaping an unwanted task that provokes anxiety.

Overall, the behavioural approach led to the development of important treatment methods like behaviour therapy and behaviour modification with all these being built on the idea that a person can "unlearn" these maladaptive behaviours or emotions.

But how does Cognitive Behavioural Therapy work for anxiety disorders specifically?

CBT FOR ANXIETY DISORDERS

Something that I really like about this book is that as the other chapters have shown us, there is an awful lot that goes into CBT, and CBT is nowhere near as straight forward as you might have previously believed since it is only now that we are getting onto CBT. As well as there is plenty more information after this chapter to deepen your knowledge even further.

Therefore, we know that anxiety disorders develop due to people believing that situations are a lot more dangerous than they really are. As well as this means psychologists need to help clients to consider alternative, less threatening explanations of their mental difficulty.

And yet, this isn't straight forward as each anxiety disorder has its own unique facets and this means a client has to learn and test these alternative ways of interpreting their experience.

Ultimately, this helps the person to make changes

to their own unique, personal situation so CBT is critical in helping them to adopt and try out these new ways of understanding themselves, their experience and most importantly their future assumptions.

How Does CBT For Anxiety Work?

The entire point of all CBT models of anxiety disorders is to help the client consider their own threatening interpretation of the experience as well as how this is maintained by their emotion and behaviour as discussed in previous chapters.

In addition, all CBT models use behavioural activation and cognitive restructuring to help the client learn alternative ways of interpreting their experience and helps them to make changes to their situation by trying out their new ways of understanding themselves, others and the world.

But that is basically where the similarities end. Every CBT model is different for each anxiety disorder.

CBT For Panic Disorder

When it comes to panic disorder, the cognitive theory proposes that people have a relatively enduring tendency to interpret a range of bodily sensations catastrophically. In other words, people with panic disorder think their bodily sensations is the end of the world and they're going to die. That's an example of how exaggerated their biased cognitive processes are.

As a result, these bodily sensations are the ones that are mainly involved in normal anxiety responses, like heart palpitations, dizziness and breathlessness, but they aren't always triggered by anxiety. Hence, the person's catastrophic interpretation involves them perceiving these sensations as indications of an immediately impending physical or mental disaster.

And come on, anyone could find this absolutely terrifying and they would rightly have a major panic attack.

Afterwards, a person might start catastrophising these sensations but that doesn't mean they should automatically be maintained and a person should have these catastrophic interpretations forever, so what maintains panic disorders?

A lot of research finds that once a person has developed a tendency to interpret body sensations in a catastrophic way, then several other processes engage and it is these processes that contribute to the maintenance of panic disorder. For example, a person's safety behaviours, imagery, emotional reasoning and their selective attention to bodily cues.

Overall, when it comes to treating panic disorder with CBT, the therapy needs to focus on cognitively restructuring these catastrophic misinterpretations, reducing their unhelpful attentional processes and helping them to reduce their safety and avoidance behaviours. This is typically done through Behavioural Experiments (my absolute favourite topic in the entire book coming up in the next chapter).

CBT For Generalised Anxiety Disorder (GAD)

Additionally, if we look at Generalised Anxiety Disorder (this will be examined more in the free bonus essay at the back of the book), the cognitive model of GAD was proposed by Wells (1995; 1997; 2000; 2009) and he proposed that the excessive worry and anxiety common in GAD was maintained by a range of factors.

For instance, Wells found that GAD was maintained by a person's hypervigilance to threats, so they're always looking out for threats and I think we can all imagine how if a person is always looking for threats they will always find them in the end.

A GAD sufferer has information processing biases like attention and interpretation biases as well that have a maintaining role too. As does the person's dysfunctional beliefs about their worry and its function. Leading people to believe that it's perfectly necessary to run through this process of avoidance because they believe it is critical to avoid future catastrophes. Despite the worry this process causes them being uncontrollable and harmful. Then like always safety seeking behaviours and avoidance also play a role in maintaining GAD.

Therefore, when a CBT therapist comes to treating GAD, they focus on the self-monitoring aspect of the person with them constantly watching out for anxiety and worry.

This is done through cognitive restructuring by challenging the beliefs they have about the likelihood and cost of the negative events, they challenge the client's dysfunctional beliefs about their worrying as well as they carry out behavioural experiments to test out their beliefs about worry.

Moreover, the therapist would help the client to reduce and disengage from their worrying and reduce their safety behaviours, like reassurance seeking.

Overall, as you can see so far and we'll come back to this point at the end of the chapter, but CBT is like a core when it comes to anxiety disorders (and pretty much all mental health conditions) and it needs to be adapted and changed to meet the needs of the client with a specific mental health condition.

No two CBTs are the same because no two conditions are the same.

What CBT Works For Social Anxiety Disorder?

To wrap up this chapter, we'll look at one final anxiety disorder because Social Anxiety Disorder is always interesting to look at. Consequently, CBT for the condition aims to help clients reduce their negative mental processes and beliefs about social situations, their overly negative view of their performance in social situations, their excessive fear of negative evaluations by others as well as their excessive importance attached to social performance.

Additionally, to put this into a perspective for those of us without social anxiety disorder can understand, whenever we go to a social situation, we always want to do well, not look like an idiot and we want people to like us at these social situations but our entire identities aren't obsessed with that and our world will not end if we make a fool of ourselves.

But that is how social situations and negative

evaluations feel to people with social anxiety disorder.

As a result, CBT for this condition seeks to reduce a person's self-focused attention, getting them to stop their safety and avoidance behaviours and get them to reduce their attentional bias to the social threat.

Ultimately, now that we've looked at CBT for three different anxiety disorders, hopefully you can see how CBT is adapted to each condition, and how there are similarities and there are some fairly stark differences as well.

And it is those differences that make this topic so fascinating to learn about.

WHAT ARE COGNITIVE INTERVENTIONS, BEHAVIOURAL EXPERIMENTS AND MORE?

This seriously has to be my favourite chapter in the entire book because I find this topic (especially behaviour experiments) just absolutely fascinating, amazing and interesting that I love to talk about them. You really are in for a brilliant treat in this chapter.

What Are Cognitive Interventions?

So far in the second part of this book, we've looked a lot at how Cognitive Behavioural Therapy works so now what we're doing is we're narrowing in on how a therapist actually goes about challenging and modifying a person's biased cognitive processes.

This is where cognitive interventions come in.

The aim of cognitive interventions are to review as well as reappraise anxiety-related thoughts and images, and like all modern clinical psychology practice (in an ideal world) this should all be based on a shared formulation between the therapist and client.

Typically, a cognitive intervention starts by tackling a person's Negative Automatic Thoughts before moving onto deeper levels of cognition, and the core beliefs are left until later in the therapy, and they're only touched if necessary.

<u>Thought Records</u>

One type of cognitive intervention is thought records and this is so much easier now for clients now that everyone has a smartphone. As well as a thought record is quite literally a person recording their thoughts and certain details about it.

These records used to be done using pen and paper but the problem with that is a person is very unlikely to do it in public because they don't want to alert people around them, they're having to record their thoughts and come on, if a person is anxiety because their biased cognitive processes are telling them people are staring at them, and they randomly get a pen and paper to start recording their thoughts. People will look at them and their biased cognitive processes will only get confirmed (to some extent).

Thankfully this is less of a problem now with thought records being largely done on people's phones and phones are so common now we don't really bat an eyelid if we see someone typing on their phone.

In addition, here are the key stages of the cognitive restructuring process that happens when a person is using a Thought Record Identification of the event.

- They connect to the feeling the thought triggered.
- They identify the Negative Automatic Thought or Image and explore its meaning. This is known as the identification of the "hot thought"
- They find evidence for the "hot thought"
- Evidence against the "hot thought"
- Write a balanced statement
- Re-evaluate their feelings

And as you can imagine the vast majority of the time, the person finds there is more evidence against the Negative Automatic Thoughts or Image then there is supporting it.

A quick teaching-only example would be a person is sitting on a train and their automatic thought tells them every one is staring at them. They record that thought and how it makes them feel very anxious and scared. Then they might realise that yes, one or two people are looking about and smiling if someone looks at them (evidence for it). Yet these people are looking at everyone and for most of the train journey they were reading their book, and all ten other people in the train carriage aren't looking at them (evidence against) so they conclude the thought wasn't correct and they shouldn't feel scared and anxious.

<u>Behavioural Experiments (BES)</u>

Now this is the section of the book I absolutely love because Behavioural Experiments are so cool, amazing and just flat out brilliant. I love learning about them and if you ever find a good video of these being done properly or you get to use them or see them in real life, you'll realise how amazing they are too.

However, for the sake of clarity, a behavioural experiment is:

"Planned experiential activities, based on experimentation or observation, which are undertaken by clients in or between sessions" (Bennett-Levy, J., Butler, G. Fennell, M., Hackmann, A., Mueller, M. & Westbrook, D., 2004).

As well as these are very powerful to combating safety behaviours and their design is directly generated from cognitive formulations of presenting problems. In other words, behavioural experiments are done to counteract the client's presenting problems as seen in a hot-cross-bun formulation, for example.

Why Use Behavioural Experiments?

Personally, I would say why wouldn't you use them, but as great as thought records are because they allow the client to become more aware of their thinking and patterns of behaviour, and even come up with their own alternatives to these thoughts and behaviours. The person can still not be fully convinced that the alternatives are true.

As a result, behavioural experiments can:

- Test a client's unhelpful existing beliefs.
- Test out their new and more helpful beliefs

- Collect information to help develop the formulation further
- They enable experiential learning. Basically learning by doing.
- Allow clients to test out theory A versus Theory B

One of the ways and something that is very common in CBT is that a client will argue forever that they know what you're saying and the alternatives are true at a logical and fact level and they "feel it in my heart" and they "know it in their head" but they still refuse to believe it.

That's why behavioural experiments are very powerful ways to get them to see what happens when they drop their safety behaviours.

Of course, I'm not saying that behavioural experiments are easy for both the therapist and the client. Since the therapist needs to design behavioural experiments so, so carefully because if one of these experiments goes wrong then you have basically just confirmed outright a person's biased cognitive errors and beliefs. That isn't what you want.

Additionally, these can be difficult for the client because your therapist is basically making you confront something you absolutely hate.

However, if you ever see get a chance to see these experiments in practice as a student then definitely watch them. Since the one I watched was with an anxious woman who believed she would have sweat pouring off her, she would be violently shaking like an earthquake and she would be tomato red when she had to talk to a stranger so the therapist filmed an interaction and it turned out the woman was completely wrong.

She wasn't bright tomato red, she wasn't shaking (you really couldn't tell she was shaking at all) and no visual sweat was coming off her. This made the woman very surprised and happy and the therapist got the woman to do the experiment twice, once with safety behaviours and one without.

And you know what happened?

The woman admitted she looked so much more personable, likeable and human when she did the experiment without her safety behaviours.

It was a very powerful and fascinating thing to watch and enjoy.

On the whole, the purpose of behavioural experiments is to get new information so the client can test the validity of their existing beliefs and cognitions. This includes them testing the content of these beliefs and cognitions and seeing the effect of their maladaptive processes. As well as behavioural experiments allow clients to create and test new, more adaptive beliefs and cognitions.

Finally, if we supply this information to anxiety disorders (the entire purpose of the book) then these experiments allow people to get new information to test the validity of the non-threatening explanation of anxiety and associated symptoms, and they help people to recognise that the anxiety-provoking situation they hate, isn't actually that dangerous in reality.

EXPOSURE THERAPY

We seriously couldn't do a book on treatments for anxiety disorders without investigating exposure therapy, and this is a therapy that is so often used in books, TV and films that I just know a lot of people would have been disappointed if I didn't write about it. And personally, I would have been disappointed too because exposure therapy is flat out brilliant.

<u>What Is Exposure Therapy?</u>

Exposure therapy is a psychological treatment that was developed to help people confront their fears. Since whenever people are fearful or scared of something, they tend to avoid the feared object, situation or activity. For example, if a person is fearful of social situations or spiders then the person will avoid said social situation and spider.

Furthermore, as we know from earlier chapters, this avoidance behaviour might help the person to reduce their feelings of fear in the short term, in the long term it can make the fear even worse. Basically, this has the complete opposite effect than intended.

As a result, in exposure therapy, psychologists create a safe environment so the client can get "exposed" to the anxiety provoking, fearful objects, situations and activities that they avoid and find fearful. If the therapy is done correctly (more on that later) then this leads to a reduction in their fearful response and avoidance behaviour.

Moreover, exposure therapy isn't some guru rubbish that doesn't have supportive literature, it has been scientifically shown to be an effective treatment or treatment component for a wide range of mental health conditions. Such as:

- Social Anxiety Disorder
- Generalized Anxiety Disorder
- Phobias
- Obsessive-Compulsive Disorder
- Panic Disorder
- Posttraumatic Stress Disorder

How Is Exposure Therapy Done?

Now this is why I really enjoy learning about exposure therapy because the therapy really has come such a long way since its beginning. Especially since when I think about Exposure Therapy I only imagine a client looking at a spider in a glass box and it then crawling up on the client's arm.

Even though I don't have a spider phobia, I seriously couldn't imagine me willingly having a massive spider crawling up my arm. That's just goes to show how amazingly brave our clients are.

However, this is only one of the ways exposure therapy is done.

The first way exposure therapy is done is by what's known as "In vivo exposure" and this is basically what I mentioned above. Since this is when you directly face the feared situation, object or activity in real life.

For example, to use a different example, if a person is terrified of horses then they might be instructed to handle a horse, or a person with social anxiety might be asked to give a speech in front of an audience.

Another method is "Imaginal Exposure". This involves a person vividly imagining the feared situation, object or activity. And a great example here is from PTSD sufferers, because they might be asked to recall and describe their traumatic experience in great detail to reduce the feelings of fear.

Penultimately, Virtual Reality (VR) can be used as a form of exposure because in some cases, VR technology can be used in cases where In Vivo exposure just isn't practical. For example, we can all see that if a person has a fear of flying then the psychologist isn't going to rent a plane and take the client flying for the hour of their therapy appointment. It would be cool if they did but that really isn't practical in the slightest.

So VR comes in very handy in cases like this, especially as the VR equipment in the psychologist office's can be used to provide the sights, smells and sounds of an aeroplane.

Finally, "Interoceptive Exposure" can be used. This is a very interesting one because it involves bringing on physical sensations that are harmless to the client but fearful. Such as, if you're working with a client with panic disorder, they might be instructed to run on the spot to make their heart speed up so the person learns that the sensation isn't dangerous.

That's brilliant because the whole "problem" with a panic disorder is that the person is fearful of the physical sensation.

What Is Graded Exposure?

Originally in my weird little notes the three next sections were later in the chapter but as you'll see that just flat out wouldn't work.

Anyway, graded exposure is an absolutely critical feature of Exposure Therapy because it involves a fear hierarchy. This is a list of a person's triggers that makes them feel afraid or anxious, and these triggers are ranked from the trigger that is least anxiety provoking to the most provoking.

For example, if you have a client that is terrified of spiders then the least anxiety provoking situation might be seeing a photo of a spider, followed by watching a video of a spider, being in the same room as a spider and then allowing a spider to crawl up your arm.

This is a good example for a hierarchy for spider phobias, but of course a real one depends on the client.

Additionally, it's important in Exposure Therapy to try and have these items by distress number (another way of saying the amount of distress it causes goes up linear) so there are no big jumps. Then the idea is to make sure the client and the therapist work their way through the list from the lowest number to the highest number also known as the most anxiety-provoking.

Also, it's a good idea to make sure the theme of the list is relevant to the goals of the therapy. Therefore, a therapist could experiment with each item several times until the client no longer feels distress in that situation.

For instance, going back to our spider example, a therapist wouldn't move from getting the client to look at images of a spider before moving onto watching a video. As well as the therapist might have the client look at images of small, medium and massive spiders to make sure the client no longer feels anxious after looking at images before moving onto the next one.

Equally, sometimes therapists might "only" keep experimenting until the distress in a given situation is about half of what it was. This makes sense because it isn't until a client reaches the top of their hierarchy that their anxiety responses are a lot better than before treatment.

That's the easiest way to explain it.

How Does Exposure Therapy Work?

This is what we all want to know because as psychology is a science, we want to know why and how something works. Therefore, there are four main mechanisms that help change to occur during a course of Exposure Therapy.

Firstly, the client goes through a process of habituation where over time, people find that their reactions to the feared objects, situations or activities decrease because of their exposure to them. This links with the challenging of their biased beliefs because if a client is being exposed to the feared object without the world ending then this helps them to learn that maybe their beliefs were wrong.

Secondly, the cognitive process of extinction occurs where exposure helps to weaken the previously learnt associations between feared objects, activities or situations and bad outcomes.

And yes, this has a lot to do with the psychology of learning, which you can read more about in *Cognitive Psychology: A Guide To Neuropsychology, Neuroscience and Cognitive Psychology*.

Thirdly, and this is something I think is so, so important in therapy work. A client learns about their own self-efficacy. Meaning the exposure helps to show the client that they're perfectly capable of confronting their own fears as well as they can manage the feelings of their anxiety.

This links to the brilliant concept of CBT Pie Charts, a very powerful and fascinating therapy tool, that I discuss more in *Clinical Psychology Reflections*

Volume 4.

Finally, exposure therapy is great for emotional processing since during the exposure, the client can learn to attach new, more realistic beliefs about feared objects, activities or situations, and they can become more comfortable with the experience of fear.

What Are The Four Rules of Exposure Therapy?

I have to admit that psychologists love rules, methods and having to do things a certain way and this is definitely true for CBT, but when it comes to Exposure Therapy, these four rules are particularly important because if a therapist doesn't stick to the rules then chances are the therapy will fail and the client will only be worst off.

Therefore, the first rule of Exposure Therapy is the exposure absolutely has to be graded. If we look back at our spider example, you seriously cannot go from getting a client to look at photos of spiders to having a spider crawling up their arm. That will end so badly and the client will never improve and yeah, it will not be pretty.

Just don't do that.

In addition, and see this as a sub-rule of the first one, when it comes to creating the Hierarchy of Anxious Situations, it's best to start with the most anxiety-provoking and then work down. Remember, this is the creation phase because if a therapist asks a client about the object that causes them the least anxiety. Chances are they will not know.

They only know the *most* anxiety-provoking one

so it's best to start there and then it breaks the ice, allowing you to ask more questions, investigate more and slowly work your way down towards the least anxiety-provoking ones.

Remember, therapy is a process and so is the creation of this hierarchy.

Secondly, these exposures have to be prolonged since the therapists need to wait until the anxiety comes down to about half of what it was before they started before they get the client to stop. Since if the therapist stops it too soon then they risk reinforcing the very behaviour they are trying to get the client to stop.

Thirdly, these exposures have to be repeated so the client should continue doing the exposure of the same activity until their pre-activity anxiety comes down to about half what it was when the therapist planned the activity.

Again, if a therapist shows a client a photo of a spider and the client starts rapidly breathing, they would wait until the rapid breathing decreases before moving on to the next task.

Finally, these exposures have to be done without distraction. The client has to be focused on these exposures and learn that their biased beliefs are not based in reality and the danger is nowhere near what they believe it is. And distractions only make this learning or unlearning even harder.

<u>Exposure And Response Prevention</u>

This next aspect is very similar to standard

graded exposure and this is when a therapist and a client work together, much like how they do in CBT, to develop a hierarchy like we saw in the last few sections and the four principles still apply.

However, the difference is that the client needs to resist the urge to respond to a compulsive desire and it is important for the client to sit with the distress until it comes down to about half.

The clearest fictional example of this is with OCD. For example, a client might have the urge to start cleaning whenever they see dirt so their compulsion might be hand cleaning so at least they are clean. In this situation, the client would have to sit with that compulsion and *not* clean their hands.

Of course, this would cause a lot of distress and anxiety but it will also show the client that nothing bad will happen to them if they don't wash their hands the second the compulsion manifests itself.

What Are The Common Difficulties With Exposure?

Of course, nothing in psychology like life is straight forward and therapy is no different. Therefore, there will be problems a therapist encounters with their clients when it comes to exposure therapy. Some of these problems include:

- The client doesn't want to get started and the therapist can't encourage them.

You cannot do a therapy if the client isn't willing to put in the work and at least try it, but exposure therapy is terrifying for people.

- Missing activities or missing steps in the hierarchy. That will almost always end badly.
- The client or therapist or both tries to do too much too soon.
- Jumping ahead in the hierarchy.
- The client doesn't drop their safety behaviours so they still believe it is their safety behaviours that are protecting them.
- Both the client and therapist have difficulties categorising activities in the hierarchy.

This is problematic because if a therapist can't categorise activities properly then it is so much harder to understand how to properly go up the hierarchy without the risk of jumping steps and trying to do too much at once.

- Stopping an activity before the anxiety drops.

How To Address Safety behaviours In Exposure Therapy?

Some of you might have realised that normally in CBT (which is completely separate from Exposure Therapy), you carry out cognitive interventions including behavioural experiments to challenge and address a person's beliefs and safety behaviours. And I'm sure there is a good argument that Exposure Therapy is a good form of cognitive intervention, but Exposure Therapy does not have a good way of addressing safety behaviours. At least from what we've seen so far.

The first step of getting rid of any safety behaviour is obviously identifying them, you can't get rid of something if you don't know what it is.

As well as we need to remember that safety behaviours try to distract us from the experience of our anxiety, and this is important because it reduces the opportunities for habituation. As well as this is why it's sometimes a very good idea to make a list of safety behaviours that might get in the way of habituation with the client.

As a result, a person might say to a therapist "I can look at spider photos if I do…"

We don't want them to say that. And whilst it is sometimes "okay" to allow a safety behaviour in order to make a jump in the hierarchy, this isn't ideal in the slightest, but when this is done, the next step should be completed without the safety behaviour before moving on to the next.

A practical example would be the one we've been using all chapter, if a client couldn't even look at a photo of a spider but we saw there was a decrease of about a quarter to a third in anxiety. Then maybe a therapist could allow them to do a safety behaviour before moving on to the next one.

Again, this really, really does come down to clinical judgement and the therapist's experience.

Overall, at the end of this great chapter, I have to admit that Exposure Therapy is definitely a serious but potentially fun therapy because we get to help our clients, and get very creative at the same time, and it is that creativity that I just love.

CONCLUSION

After reading this book and looking at so many amazing topics and aspects of both anxiety disorders and CBT, I have to say this has been a really fun journey to learn about and explore these topics. Since a lot of people believe that anxiety disorders are just that, they are simply disorders that need to be fixed.

Of course, that is very blaming language and it misses the most important aspects of all mental health conditions. It is that behind the label, behind the symptoms and behind the maladaptive coping mechanisms, is a real flesh and blood person.

And that is why the stuff in this book and anxiety disorders and CBT is so amazingly critical, because now you know the stuff, even at an introductory level, it helps you in your own personal journey to become a clinical psychologist (if that's what you want to do) so you can help brilliant people that want you to help them.

CBT gives you the tools and techniques to help

change a person's life, decrease their psychological distress and improve their lives.

That is why I love this topic and that's what I want to conclude this book with. I know you to walk away from this book feeling a certain level of empowerment because of course, depending on where you are in your psychology journey, be you an undergraduate, Masters or DClinPsych student. I want you to know that you have the power to help people if you just keep learning, developing your skills and maintain your passion for this amazing profession.

Current and future psychologists have the power to do so much good in the world and it is that passion, love and hunger to learn that truly sustains this magical profession.

So please, keep learning, keep enjoying psychology and look forward to treating and helping the great people that have the courage to walk through our therapy room doors.

Because our profession really can be the most rewarding one on the planet in my very, very biased opinion.

REFERENCES

Carpenter, J. K., Andrews, L. A., Witcraft, S. M., Powers, M. B., Smits, J. A., & Hofmann, S. G. (2018). Cognitive Behavioral Therapy For Anxiety And Related Disorders: A Meta-Analysis Of Randomized Placebo-Controlled Trials. *Depression & Anxiety*, 35, 502–514.

Carr, A. & Mcnulty, M. (Eds.) (2016). *The Handbook Of Adult Clinical Psychology: An Evidence-Based Approach* (2nd Ed.) Hove: Routledge. Chapters 13 - 18.

Clark, D. M. (1986). A Cognitive Approach To Panic. *Behaviour Research & Therapy*, 24, 461-470.

Davey, G. (2014). *Psychopathology: Research, Assessment And Treatment In Clinical Psychology* (2nd Ed.). Chichester: Wiley. Chapter 6.

Hirsch, C. R., Mathews, A., Lequertier, B., Perman, G., & Hayes, S. (2013). Characteristics Of Worry In Generalized Anxiety Disorder. *Journal Of Behavior Therapy And Experimental Psychiatry*, 44, 388-395.

Kennerley, H., Kirk, J. & Westbrook, D. (2016). *An Introduction To Cognitive Behaviour Therapy: Skills And*

Applications (3rd Ed.). London: Sage. Chapters 1-11 (CBT Approaches & Techniques); Chapter 14 (Anxiety Disorders).

Rapee, R. M. & Heimberg, R. G. (1997). A Cognitive-Behavioral Model Of Anxiety In Social Phobia. *Behaviour Research & Therapy*, 35, 741-756.

Salkovskis, P. M. (1991). The Importance Of Behaviour In The Maintenance Of Anxiety And Panic: A Cognitive Account. *Behavioural Psychotherapy*, 19, 6-19.

Salkovskis, P. M. (1999). Understanding And Treating Obsessive-Compulsive Disorder. *Behaviour Research And Therapy*, 37, S29-S52.

Wells, A. (1997). *Cognitive Therapy Of Anxiety Disorders: A Practice Manual And Conceptual Guide.* Chichester: Wiley.

Compare the effectiveness of Cognitive Behaviour Therapy (CBT) with Mindfulness-Based Cognitive Therapy For Generalised Anxiety Disorder.

Anxiety disorders are a group of psychological conditions and the most common of all conditions (Davey et al., 2015) characterised by feelings of danger and anxiety in response to threatening stimuli and situations (Davey et al., 2015). Generalised Anxiety Disorder (GAD) is one type in this group of conditions with a prevalence rate differing between occupation, country and age. For example, during a study exploring the impact of COVID-19 on mental health 35.1% of Chinese people was diagnosed with GAD (Huang and Zhao, 2020) but a more general prevalence rate for a western country is 5.9% (McManus et al., 2016). GAD separates itself from other anxiety disorders because GAD sufferers exhibit an excessive concern in several important areas of daily functioning and intolerance of uncertainty (Borza, 2022) not found in other anxiety disorders. Also it is characterised by the DSM-5 as presenting excessive anxiety, worry about a wide range of events, activities or topics, is clearly excessive and has been present for at least 6 months (APA, 2013). GAD does not only result in chronic anxiety and worry (DeMartini et al., 2019) but GAD causes increased risk of suicide, cardiovascular-related events and death (DeMartini et al., 2019). These negative psychological and physical health outcomes mean treatment is critical. Therefore, this essay will investigate the effectiveness of Cognitive Behavioural Therapy (CBT) compared against Mindfulness-Based Cognitive Therapy (MBCT) in the treatment of Generalised Anxiety Disorder by introducing each psychotherapy, exploring their methodologies, strengths and weaknesses before concluding which therapy could be best. Further, this essay highlights the lack of direct comparison between CBT and MBCT with Apolinario-Hagen et al. (2020) being the only major comparison review found.

One treatment method for GAD is Cognitive Behavioural Therapy (Broza, 2022; Davey et al., 2015). This psychotherapy extends behavioural therapies, like exposure therapy, by tackling cognitions allowing anxiety to thrive since cognitive theory argues anxiety is maintained by a person's perception of stimuli being more threatening than it objectively is (Davey et al., 2015; Fenn and Bryne, 2013). Therefore, based on Beck and Emery (1985), CBT for anxiety seeks to weaken the threatening appraisal of stimuli and strengthen coping appraisals to decrease this anxiety (Davey et al., 2015). Typically, this is done through psychoeducation, experimenting with new behaviours, like approach rather than avoid behaviours and the development of functional analysis skills helping clients to identify the when, where and what of their anxiety and therapists can use this to introduce other important psychological topics later in the therapy (Borza, 2022). A plethora of research demonstrates the effectiveness of CBT treating GAD (Borza, 2022) and this causes CBT to be argued as one of the most researched treatments for anxiety disorders (Carpenter et al., 2018), resulting in a decrease in worry and is still effective 6 months after treatment completion. Overall, CBT is an effective treatment for GAD based on a wide range of literature (Borza, 2022)

Additionally, meta-analyses demonstrate CBT is a highly effective treatment for a multitude of mental health conditions (Butler et al., 2006; Cuijpers et al., 2014; Hall et al., 2016; Hofmann et al., 2012; Olatunji et al., 2010) demonstrating a strong evidence base for the treatment in anxiety disorder specifically (Apolinario-Hagen et al., 2020; Van Dis et al., 2020) with Bulter et al. (2006) finding CBT shows large effect size in a range of anxiety disorders including GAD. This finding of moderate to large effect sizes has been supported with additional studies (Apolinario-Hagen et al., 2020; Carpenter et al., 2018; Deacon et al., 2004; Olatunji et al., 2010; Reinholt and Krogh, 2014). Also, CBT has been found to treat GAD more effectively than yoga and stress-management education programmes (Simon et al., 2020). An advantage of CBT over other interventions is its devotion to the scientific method since whilst clinical judgement is used frequently in CBT (Borza, 2022) several measures are used to empirically evaluate the clinical improvement of the client. For instance, Anxiety and Related Disorders Interview Schedule for DSM-4 (Brown et al., 2014), Anxiety

Disorder Interview Schedule For DSM-4 Child Version (Silverman et al, 1996) amongst others (Dugas et al., 1995; First, 1997; Spitzer et al., 2006). On the whole, CBT is demonstrated in the literature to be a highly effective treatment for GAD focusing on the empirical method (Borza, 2022) due to a range of factors (Davey et al., 2015). For example, its large effect sizes mean there were large differences in the treatment outcomes for CBT groups and control groups or those of additional interventions (Apolinario-Hagen et al., 2020) and these randomised-controlled trials (RCT), like Hofmann and Smifs (2008), are backed up with real-world setting research supporting CBT as one of the most effective treatment interventions for anxiety disorders (Stewart and Chambless, 2009). Hence, giving CBT strong ecological validity in naturalistic and controlled-settings due to its high-quality research (Otte, 2022).

Building upon the success of "first-wave" CBT, "Third wave" CB therapies address the meta-cognitive level of mental health conditions by changing the context and function of maladaptive psychological processes related to a client's feelings and thoughts (Hofmann et al., 2010, Kabat-Zinn, 2003). These newer therapies focus more on the context and not pathology of the conditions compared to behavioural therapies (Hayes and Hofmann, 2017; Hofmann et al., 2010), including Mindfulness-Based Cognitive Therapy (MBCT) (Ghahari et al., 2020; Segal et al., 2018). MBCT works by adding cognitive elements to mindfulness-based programmes using an 8-week format and several mindfulness-based components (Apolinario-Hagen et al., 2020; Hofmann et al., 2010). Also MBCT utilities condition-specific psychoeducation (Xie et al., 2014) and the therapy aims to help clients learn to control the shift between focused attention (mindfulness) and unfocused attention (autopilot modus) in daily activities (Teasdale et al., 1995). This essay must note the wording "third wave" therapies has become controversial (Hayes and Hofmann, 2017) since Hofmann et al (2010) suggests this term is misleading due to the slight differences in the theoretical base and procedures between these "waves" of therapy. Hofmann argues all waves belong to the same CBT family and are not separate from each other.

However, unlike in CBT, the mechanisms of change are relatively understood and explained by the cognitive vulnerability model as repeated automated negative thoughts become associated with a depressed state triggering and increasing risk of relapse with each new depression episode (MacKenzie and Kocovski, 2016; Kuyken et al., 2010; Teasdale et al., 2000, Teasdale et al., 1995), and focuses on developing a client's mindfulness (Alsubaie et al., 2017, van der Velden et al., 2015), compassion (van der Velden et al., 2015), emotional regulation and reactivity (Gu et al., 2015) and meta-cognitive awareness (van der Velden et al., 2015). Also unlike CBT, MBCT focuses on fostering a client's awareness about their personal relationship to their feelings and thoughts (the meta-cognitive level) and not changing of content of these thoughts (Sipe and Eisendrath, 2012).

As GAD often has a chronic course, having the condition continuously or having it again and again (Merriam-Webster, 1995), and is the least successfully treated form of anxiety (Crane, 2017; Evans, 2016; Ghahari et al., 2020; Starcevic and Castle, 2016), Evans (2016) proposed an 8-week GAD-specific form of MBCT as an alternative to CBT based on MBCT for major depression (Segal, 2002). There is a plethora of studies showing positive and beneficial effects of MBCT for GAD (Craigie et al., 2008; Evans et al., 2008). For example, MBCT was conducted on a group of 24 pregnant women, 17 had GAD, and by the end of the programme only 1 met the diagnostic criteria for GAD (Goodman et al., 2014). Wong et al. (2016) demonstrated the effectiveness of MBCT and psychoeducation groups reducing anxiety symptoms in GAD clinical samples and a randomised control trial by Kim et al. (2009) showed MBCT was effective in GAD clients when used in conjunction with pharmacotherapy. MBCT is feasible, effective and affordable as well in non-WEIRD samples too as supported by Sado et al. (2018). Overall, research demonstrates MBCT can be an effective alternative to CBT for GAD as supported by a range of evidence from different clinical settings and MBCT improves on CBT by focusing on the meta-cognitive level and focusing less on pathology by using yoga and other mindfulness-based activities. Therefore, making this psychotherapy a more attractive option for people delaying and putting off therapy (Apolinario-Hagen et al., 2020).

Moreover, CBT is not perfect and there is always room for improvement in psychological interventions. Since whilst CBT has strong empirical basis (Otte, 2022), there are literature weaknesses. For example, the majority of CBT research is carried out with rigorous procedures in academic settings because this is the best research design to answer efficacy questions around CBT (Simon et al., 2020), but these studies might not fully generalise to how CBT is delivered in the real world. As a result, future work could use a community-based effectiveness design to counter this potential issue (Simon et al., 2020). Also, whilst the naturalistic research issue was addressed in Otte (2022), it is still critical to recognise the drawbacks of research in academic settings and how it decreases the ecological validity and generalisability of psychological research. Another weakness of CBT research is there is a literature gap surrounding the advantage of CBT over active controls, other treatments and the long-term assessment of CBT in GAD (Cuijpers et al., 2014; Hall et al., 2016). This is important because of the often chronic course of GAD (Apolinario-Hagen et al., 2020). Therefore, these limitations have the potential to undermine the effectiveness of CBT for GAD because without sufficient amounts of ecologically valid research, clinical psychologists cannot say with certainty CBT is effective for GAD in the real world, so researchers must be mindful in the creation of their studies to maintain high levels of validity. Also, without greater research into CBT versus active controls, we will not know with empirical certainty if CBT itself works for treating GAD or the act of doing something is what leads to a reduction in GAD symptoms.

Building upon this and linking this to MBCT, CBT therapies have equal or near-equal effectiveness (Kaczkurkin and Foa, 2022) so whilst both therapies are effective at treating GAD, it suggests the commonalities between these interventions are more important than meta-cognitive components of MBCT and the cognitive-behavioural focus of CBT, for example. However, few studies have examined or attempted to identify the commonalities between CBT and MBCT in particular (Kaczkurkin and Foa, 2022). Therefore, this represents researchers with an important yet underdeveloped area of clinical treatment and this is another gap in the literature. This issue is worse for MBCT because the mechanisms of therapeutic change are still being understood so this therapy requires more deconstructive studies to help delineate the active components of therapeutic change within MBCT (Sipe and Eisendrath, 2012), with this essay proposing these deconstructive studies would be helpful to CBT to better understand and identify the commonalities within the CBT family of therapies as well. This is problematic for CBT and MBCT because without an understanding of the commonalities making effective treatment possible then clinical psychologists could be lacking vital tools at their disposal, so additional studies capable of dismantling effective treatments for GAD to find commonalities are needed (Kaczkurkin and Foa, 2022). Also, unlike CBT, MBCT studies are commonly combined with other treatments, pharmacology or behavioural, this only increases the difficulty in determining specific effects of MBCT (Apolinario-Hagen et al., 2020). Consequently, clinical psychologists could argue MBCT might have no effect on GAD unlike CBT because there is a lack of clear research investigating the effects of only MBCT on GAD. This is not a problem for the CBT literature.

Additionally, both CBT and MBCT have a long-term research problem in their literature. Neither psychological intervention for GAD uses longitudinal studies so the longer-term effectiveness of each psychotherapy is relatively unknown. One study examining long-term effectiveness is Van Dis et al. (2019)'s meta-analysis demonstrating CBT was effective at treating a multitude of anxiety disorders, including GAD, and relapse rates within 12 months was 0% to 12%, but few studies looked further. Consequently, whilst both CBT and MBCT benefit from a few studies examining long-term effectiveness, both literatures require more longitudinal studies to have a deeper, more complete understanding of the long-term implications of these psychotherapies. Since this lack of long-term research means clinical psychologists cannot state with empirical certainty nor that these therapies work in the long term, especially for more than 12 months.

Although, there are methodological issues CBT does not have but MBCT does. For example, whilst Otte (2022) highlighted the strong empirical foundation of CBT, MBCT lacks both the rigour and quantity of this research because the MBCT literature is overwhelmed with uncontrolled pilot studies (Apolinario-Hagen et al., 2020). Resulting in MBCT researchers not having the statistical power, sample size and larger scale testing to back up their claims of MBCT's empirical effectiveness, similar to what Herdson et al. (under submission) examines about the Gamification of Autism. Hence, casting doubt on the scientific basis of MBCT as a treatment for GAD.

Finally, whilst CBT makes plentiful use of RCT, the literature lacks RCTs in mindfulness-based interventions for GAD (Apolinario-Hagen et al., 2020). Therefore, MBCT does not have amounts of studies controlling for additional factors and influences that are not under experimental control (Bhide et al., 2018) and the mindfulness-based literature does not benefit from RCT research being the most robust and empirical methodology establishing whether a cause-and-effect relationship exists (Bhide et al., 2018). Overall, this lack of RCT undermines the effectiveness of MBCT for GAD because there is minimal research supporting the notion MBCT *causes* a reduction in GAD symptoms. This problem would be overcome by the use of more RCT in research therefore a plethora of research using RCT is needed to enhance the empirical basis of MBCT, something that has not changed in over a decade as supported by Sipe and Eisendrath (2012).

This essay set out to compare the effectiveness of CBT with MBCT for GAD and concludes CBT is the better treatment for GAD. Whilst there is a multitude of evidence highlighting the effectiveness of MBCT for GAD (Craigie et al., 2008; Evans et al., 2008), there is more empirically rigorous and higher quality research showing CBT is more effective for treating GAD (Otte, 2022). Also, there are less severe methodological issues with CBT when compared to MBCT, for example MBCT uses fewer full-scale studies and more pilot studies (Apolinario-Hagen et al., 2020), the literature uses fewer RCT studies (Apolinario-Hagen et al., 2020; Sipe and Eisendrath, 2012) and MBCT requires more deconstructive studies to fully understand the therapeutic change occurring in the therapy (Kaczkurkin and Foa, 2022). This essay acknowledges the weaknesses of CBT like the lack of longitudinal studies and studies identifying the commonalities between CBT therapies, but in comparison to the issues of MBCT literature, these issues are less stark. Therefore, CBT has an empirically stronger and more robust research basis hence this essay's conclusion of CBT being more effective than MBCT for the treatment of GAD.

REFERENCES

Alsubaie, M., Abbott, R., Dunn, B., Dickens, C., Keil, T. F., Henley, W., & Kuyken, W. (2017). Mechanisms of action in mindfulness-based cognitive therapy (MBCT) and mindfulness-based stress reduction (MBSR) in people with physical and/or psychological conditions: A systematic review. *Clinical Psychology Review, 55*, 74-91.

American Psychiatric Association. (2013). Diagnostic and statistical manual of mental disorders (5th ed.). https://doi.org/10.1176/appi.books.9780890425596.

Apolinário-Hagen, J., Drüge, M., & Fritsche, L. (2020). Cognitive behavioral therapy, mindfulness-based cognitive therapy and acceptance commitment therapy for anxiety disorders: integrating traditional with digital treatment approaches. *Anxiety Disorders: Rethinking and Understanding Recent Discoveries*, 291-329.

Beck, A. T. & Emery, G.(1985). *Anxiety disorders and phobias: A cognitive perspective*. Basic Books/Hachette Book Group.

Bhide, A., Shah, P. S., & Acharya, G. (2018). A simplified guide to randomized controlled trials. *Acta*

Obstetricia Et Gynecologica Scandinavica, *97*(4), 380–387. https://doi.org/10.1111/aogs.13309

Borza, L. (2022). Cognitive-behavioral therapy for generalized anxiety. *Dialogues in clinical neuroscience*.

Brown, T. A., & Barlow, D. H. (2014). *Anxiety and related disorders interview schedule for DSM-5 (ADIS-5)-adult and lifetime version: Clinician manual*. Oxford University Press.

Butler, A. C., Chapman, J. E., Forman, E. M., & Beck, A. T. (2006). The empirical status of cognitive-behavioral therapy: A review of meta-analyses. *Clinical Psychology Review*, *26*(1), 17-31.

Carpenter, J. K., Andrews, L. A., Witcraft, S. M., Powers, M. B., Smits, J. A., & Hofmann, S. G. (2018). Cognitive behavioral therapy for anxiety and related disorders: A meta-analysis of randomized placebo-controlled trials. *Depression And Anxiety*, *35*(6), 502-514.

Craigie, M. A., Rees, C. S., Marsh, A., & Nathan, P. (2008). Mindfulness-based cognitive therapy for generalized anxiety disorder: A preliminary evaluation. *Behavioural and Cognitive Psychotherapy*, *36*(5), 553-568.

Crane, R. (2017). *Mindfulness-Based Cognitive Therapy: Distinctive Features*. Routledge.

Cuijpers, P., Sijbrandij, M., Koole, S., Huibers, M., Berking, M., & Andersson, G. (2014). Psychological treatment of generalized anxiety disorder: a meta-analysis. *Clinical Psychology Review*, *34*(2), 130-140.

Davey, G., Lake, N., & Whittington, A. (Eds.). (2015). *Clinical Psychology*. Routledge.

Deacon, B. J., & Abramowitz, J. S. (2004).

Cognitive and behavioral treatments for anxiety disorders: A review of meta-analytic findings. *Journal Of Clinical Psychology, 60*(4), 429-441.

DeMartini, J., Patel, G., & Fancher, T. L. (2019). Generalized anxiety disorder. *Annals Of Internal Medicine, 170*(7), ITC49-ITC64.

Dugas, M. J., Freeston, M. H., Lachance, S., Provencher, M., & Ladouceur, R. (1995, July). The Worry and Anxiety Questionnaire: Initial validation in non-clinical and clinical samples. In *Comunicación presentada en el World Congress of Behavioral and Cognitive Therapie. Copenhague, Denmark.*

Evans, S. (2016). Mindfulness-based cognitive therapy for generalized anxiety disorder. *Mindfulness-Based Cognitive Therapy: Innovative Applications*, 145-154.

Evans, S., Ferrando, S., Findler, M., Stowell, C., & Smart, C. 8c Haglin, D.(2008). Mindfulness-based cognitive therapy for generalized anxiety disorder. *Journal of Anxiety Disorders, 22*(4), 716-721.

Fenn, K., & Byrne, M. (2013). The key principles of cognitive behavioural therapy. *InnovAiT, 6*(9), 579-585.

First, M. B. (1997). Structured clinical interview for DSM-IV axis I disorders. *Biometrics Research Department.*

Ghahari, S., Mohammadi-Hasel, K., Malakouti, S. K., & Roshanpajouh, M. (2020). Mindfulness-based cognitive therapy for generalised anxiety disorder: a systematic review and meta-analysis. *East Asian Archives of Psychiatry, 30*(2), 52-56.

Goodman, J. H., Guarino, A., Chenausky, K., Klein, L., Prager, J., Petersen, R., ... & Freeman, M. (2014). CALM Pregnancy: results of a pilot study of mindfulness-based cognitive therapy for perinatal anxiety. *Archives of Women's Mental Health, 17*, 373-387.

Gu, J., Strauss, C., Bond, R., & Cavanagh, K. (2015). How do mindfulness-based cognitive therapy and mindfulness-based stress reduction improve mental health and wellbeing? A systematic review and meta-analysis of mediation studies. *Clinical Psychology Review, 37*, 1-12.

Hall, J., Kellett, S., Berrios, R., Bains, M. K., & Scott, S. (2016). Efficacy of cognitive behavioral therapy for generalized anxiety disorder in older adults: systematic review, meta-analysis, and meta-regression. *The American Journal of Geriatric Psychiatry, 24*(11), 1063-1073.

Hayes, S. C., & Hofmann, S. G. (2017). The third wave of cognitive behavioral therapy and the rise of process-based care. *World Psychiatry, 16*(3), 245.

Herdson, O., Whiteley, C., Lashgari, E., Razzaghi, M., & Javadi, A. (2022) Working Towards Sampling and Methodological Guidelines for ASD Gamification Interventions: A Systematic Review. (Manuscript Submitted For Publication).

Hofmann, S. G., Asnaani, A., Vonk, I. J., Sawyer, A. T., & Fang, A. (2012). The efficacy of cognitive behavioral therapy: A review of meta-analyses. *Cognitive Therapy And Research, 36*, 427-440.

Hofmann, S. G., Sawyer, A. T., & Fang, A. (2010). The empirical status of the "new wave" of cognitive behavioral therapy. *Psychiatric Clinics, 33*(3), 701-710.

Huang, Y., & Zhao, N. (2020). Generalized anxiety disorder, depressive symptoms and sleep quality during COVID-19 outbreak in China: a web-based cross-sectional survey. *Psychiatry Research, 288*, 112954.

Kabat-Zinn, J. (2003). Mindfulness-based interventions in context: past, present, and future.

Kaczkurkin, A. N., & Foa, E. B. (2015). Cognitive-behavioral therapy for anxiety disorders: an update on the empirical evidence. *Dialogues In Clinical Neuroscience*, *17*(3), 337–346. https://doi.org/10.31887/DCNS.2015.17.3/akaczkurkin

Kim, Y. W., Lee, S. H., Choi, T. K., Suh, S. Y., Kim, B., Kim, C. M., ... & Yook, K. H. (2009). Effectiveness of mindfulness-based cognitive therapy as an adjuvant to pharmacotherapy in patients with panic disorder or generalized anxiety disorder. *Depression and Anxiety*, *26*(7), 601-606.

Kuyken, W., Watkins, E., Holden, E., White, K., Taylor, R. S., Byford, S., ... & Dalgleish, T. (2010). How does mindfulness-based cognitive therapy work?. *Behaviour Research And Therapy*, *48*(11), 1105-1112.

MacKenzie, M. B., & Kocovski, N. L. (2016). Mindfulness-based cognitive therapy for depression: trends and developments. *Psychology Research And Behavior Management*, 125-132.

Merriam-Webster, Inc. (1995). *Merriam-webster's medical dictionary*. Merriam-Webster.

Olatunji, B. O., Cisler, J. M., & Deacon, B. J. (2010). Efficacy of cognitive behavioral therapy for anxiety disorders: a review of meta-analytic findings. *Psychiatric Clinics*, *33*(3), 557-577.

Otte, C. (2022). Cognitive behavioral therapy in anxiety disorders: current state of the evidence. *Dialogues In Clinical Neuroscience*.

Reinholt, N., & Krogh, J. (2014). Efficacy of transdiagnostic cognitive behaviour therapy for anxiety disorders: a systematic review and meta-analysis of published outcome studies. *Cognitive Behaviour Therapy*, *43*(3), 171-184.

Sado, M., Park, S., Ninomiya, A., Sato, Y., Fujisawa, D., Shirahase, J., & Mimura, M. (2018). Feasibility study of mindfulness-based cognitive therapy for anxiety disorders in a Japanese setting. *BMC Research Notes*, *11*(1), 1-7.

Segal, Z., Williams, M., & Teasdale, J. (2018). *Mindfulness-Based Cognitive Therapy For Depression*. Guilford publications.

Segal, Z., Williams, M., & Teasdale, J. (2018). *Mindfulness-based cognitive therapy for depression*. Guilford publications.

Silverman, W. K., & Albano, A. M. (1996). *Anxiety disorders interview schedule for DSM-IV: Child version*. Oxford University Press.

Simon, N. M., Hofmann, S. G., Rosenfield, D., Hoeppner, S. S., Hoge, E. A., Bui, E., & Khalsa, S. B. S. (2021). Efficacy of yoga vs cognitive behavioral therapy vs stress education for the treatment of generalized anxiety disorder: a randomized clinical trial. *JAMA Psychiatry*, *78*(1), 13-20.

Sipe, W. E., & Eisendrath, S. J. (2012). Mindfulness-based cognitive therapy: theory and practice. *The Canadian Journal of Psychiatry*, *57*(2), 63-69.

Spitzer, R. L., Kroenke, K., Williams, J. B., & Löwe, B. (2006). A brief measure for assessing generalized anxiety disorder: the GAD-7. *Archives Of Internal Medicine*, *166*(10), 1092-1097.

Starcevic, V., & Castle, D.J. (2016). Chapter 24 – Anxiety Disorders.

Stewart, R. E., & Chambless, D. L. (2009). Cognitive–behavioral therapy for adult anxiety disorders in clinical practice: A meta-analysis of effectiveness studies. *Journal of consulting and clinical psychology*, *77*(4), 595.

Teasdale, J. D., Segal, Z. V., Williams, J. M. G., Ridgeway, V. A., Soulsby, J. M., & Lau, M. A. (2000). Prevention of relapse/recurrence in major depression by mindfulness-based cognitive therapy. *Journal Of Consulting And Clinical Psychology*, *68*(4), 615.

Teasdale, J. D., Segal, Z., & Williams, J. M. G. (1995). How does cognitive therapy prevent depressive relapse and why should attentional control (mindfulness) training help?. *Behaviour Research And Therapy*, *33*(1), 25-39.

van der Velden, A. M., Kuyken, W., Wattar, U., Crane, C., Pallesen, K. J., Dahlgaard, J., ... & Piet, J. (2015). A systematic review of mechanisms of change in mindfulness-based cognitive therapy in the treatment of recurrent major depressive disorder. *Clinical Psychology Review*, *37*, 26-39.

Van Dis, E. A., Van Veen, S. C., Hagenaars, M. A., Batelaan, N. M., Bockting, C. L., Van Den Heuvel, R. M., ... & Engelhard, I. M. (2020). Long-term outcomes of cognitive behavioral therapy for anxiety-related disorders: a systematic review and meta-analysis. *JAMA Psychiatry*, *77*(3), 265-273.

Wong, S. Y. S., Yip, B. H. K., Mak, W. W. S., Mercer, S., Cheung, E. Y. L., Ling, C. Y. M., ... & Ma, H. S. W. (2016). Mindfulness-based cognitive therapy v. group psychoeducation for people with generalised anxiety disorder: randomised controlled trial. *The British Journal of Psychiatry*, *209*(1), 68-75.

Xie, J. F., Zhou, J. D., Gong, L. N., Iennaco, J. D., & Ding, S. Q. (2014). Mindfulness-based cognitive therapy in the intervention of psychiatric disorders: A review. *International Journal Of Nursing Sciences, 1*(2), 232-239.

https://www.subscribepage.com/psychologyboxset

CHECK OUT THE PSYCHOLOGY WORLD
PODCAST FOR MORE PSYCHOLOGY
INFORMATION!
AVAILABLE ON ALL MAJOR PODCAST APPS.

About the author:

Connor Whiteley is the author of over 60 books in the sci-fi fantasy, nonfiction psychology and books for writer's genre and he is a Human Branding Speaker and Consultant.

He is a passionate warhammer 40,000 reader, psychology student and author.

Who narrates his own audiobooks and he hosts The Psychology World Podcast.

All whilst studying Psychology at the University of Kent, England.

Also, he was a former Explorer Scout where he gave a speech to the Maltese President in August 2018 and he attended Prince Charles' 70th Birthday Party at Buckingham Palace in May 2018.

Plus, he is a self-confessed coffee lover!

All books in 'An Introductory Series':
Careers In Psychology
Psychology of Suicide
Dementia Psychology
Clinical Psychology Reflections Volume 4
Forensic Psychology of Terrorism And Hostage-Taking
Forensic Psychology of False Allegations
Year In Psychology
CBT For Anxiety
CBT For Depression
Applied Psychology
BIOLOGICAL PSYCHOLOGY 3RD EDITION
COGNITIVE PSYCHOLOGY THIRD EDITION
SOCIAL PSYCHOLOGY- 3RD EDITION
ABNORMAL PSYCHOLOGY 3RD EDITION
PSYCHOLOGY OF RELATIONSHIPS- 3RD EDITION
DEVELOPMENTAL PSYCHOLOGY 3RD EDITION
HEALTH PSYCHOLOGY
RESEARCH IN PSYCHOLOGY
A GUIDE TO MENTAL HEALTH AND TREATMENT AROUND THE WORLD- A GLOBAL LOOK AT DEPRESSION
FORENSIC PSYCHOLOGY
THE FORENSIC PSYCHOLOGY OF THEFT, BURGLARY AND OTHER CRIMES AGAINST PROPERTY
CRIMINAL PROFILING: A FORENSIC

PSYCHOLOGY GUIDE TO FBI PROFILING AND GEOGRAPHICAL AND STATISTICAL PROFILING.
CLINICAL PSYCHOLOGY
FORMULATION IN PSYCHOTHERAPY
PERSONALITY PSYCHOLOGY AND INDIVIDUAL DIFFERENCES
CLINICAL PSYCHOLOGY REFLECTIONS VOLUME 1
CLINICAL PSYCHOLOGY REFLECTIONS VOLUME 2
Clinical Psychology Reflections Volume 3
CULT PSYCHOLOGY
Police Psychology

A Psychology Student's Guide To University
How Does University Work?
A Student's Guide To University And Learning
University Mental Health and Mindset

Other books by Connor Whiteley:

Bettie English Private Eye Series
A Very Private Woman
The Russian Case
A Very Urgent Matter
A Case Most Personal
Trains, Scots and Private Eyes
The Federation Protects

Lord of War Origin Trilogy:
Not Scared Of The Dark
Madness
Burn Them All

The Fireheart Fantasy Series
Heart of Fire
Heart of Lies
Heart of Prophecy
Heart of Bones
Heart of Fate

City of Assassins (Urban Fantasy)
City of Death
City of Marytrs
City of Pleasure
City of Power

<u>Agents of The Emperor</u>
Return of The Ancient Ones
Vigilance
Angels of Fire
Kingmaker
The Eight
The Lost Generation
Hunt
Emperor's Council
Speaker of Treachery
Birth Of The Empire
Terraforma

<u>The Rising Augusta Fantasy Adventure Series</u>
Rise To Power
Rising Walls
Rising Force
Rising Realm

<u>Lord Of War Trilogy (Agents of The Emperor)</u>
Not Scared Of The Dark
Madness
Burn It All Down

<u>Gay Romance Novellas</u>
Breaking, Nursing, Repairing A Broken Heart
Jacob And Daniel
Fallen For A Lie
Spying And Weddings

The Garro Series- Fantasy/Sci-fi

GARRO: GALAXY'S END
GARRO: RISE OF THE ORDER
GARRO: END TIMES
GARRO: SHORT STORIES
GARRO: COLLECTION
GARRO: HERESY
GARRO: FAITHLESS
GARRO: DESTROYER OF WORLDS
GARRO: COLLECTIONS BOOK 4-6
GARRO: MISTRESS OF BLOOD
GARRO: BEACON OF HOPE
GARRO: END OF DAYS

Winter Series- Fantasy Trilogy Books

WINTER'S COMING
WINTER'S HUNT
WINTER'S REVENGE
WINTER'S DISSENSION

Miscellaneous:

RETURN
FREEDOM
SALVATION
Reflection of Mount Flame
The Masked One
The Great Deer
English Independence

OTHER SHORT STORIES BY CONNOR WHITELEY

<u>Mystery Short Story Collections</u>
Criminally Good Stories Volume 1: 20 Detective Mystery Short Stories
Criminally Good Stories Volume 2: 20 Private Investigator Short Stories
Criminally Good Stories Volume 3: 20 Crime Fiction Short Stories
Criminally Good Stories Volume 4: 20 Science Fiction and Fantasy Mystery Short Stories
Criminally Good Stories Volume 5: 20 Romantic Suspense Short Stories

<u>Mystery Short Stories:</u>
Protecting The Woman She Hated
Finding A Royal Friend
Our Woman In Paris
Corrupt Driving
A Prime Assassination
Jubilee Thief
Jubilee, Terror, Celebrations
Negative Jubilation
Ghostly Jubilation
Killing For Womenkind
A Snowy Death
Miracle Of Death
A Spy In Rome
The 12:30 To St Pancreas
A Country In Trouble

A Smokey Way To Go
A Spicy Way To GO
A Marketing Way To Go
A Missing Way To Go
A Showering Way To Go
Poison In The Candy Cane
Christmas Innocence
You Better Watch Out
Christmas Theft
Trouble In Christmas
Smell of The Lake
Problem In A Car
Theft, Past and Team
Embezzler In The Room
A Strange Way To Go
A Horrible Way To Go
Ann Awful Way To Go
An Old Way To Go
A Fishy Way To Go
A Pointy Way To Go
A High Way To Go
A Fiery Way To Go
A Glassy Way To Go
A Chocolatey Way To Go
Kendra Detective Mystery Collection Volume 1
Kendra Detective Mystery Collection Volume 2
Stealing A Chance At Freedom
Glassblowing and Death
Theft of Independence
Cookie Thief

Marble Thief
Book Thief
Art Thief
Mated At The Morgue
The Big Five Whoopee Moments
Stealing An Election
Mystery Short Story Collection Volume 1
Mystery Short Story Collection Volume 2
Criminal Performance
Candy Detectives
Key To Birth In The Past

Science Fiction Short Stories:
Temptation
Superhuman Autospy
Blood In The Redwater
All Is Dust
Vigil
Emperor Forgive Us
Their Brave New World
Gummy Bear Detective
The Candy Detective
What Candies Fear
The Blurred Image
Shattered Legions
The First Rememberer
Life of A Rememberer
System of Wonder
Lifesaver
Remarkable Way She Died

The Interrogation of Annabella Stormic
Blade of The Emperor
Arbiter's Truth
Computation of Battle
Old One's Wrath
Puppets and Masters
Ship of Plague
Interrogation
Edge of Failure
One Way Choice
Acceptable Losses
Balance of Power
Good Idea At The Time
Escape Plan
Escape In The Hesitation
Inspiration In Need
Singing Warriors
Knowledge is Power
Killer of Polluters
Climate of Death
The Family Mailing Affair
Defining Criminality
The Martian Affair
A Cheating Affair
The Little Café Affair
Mountain of Death
Prisoner's Fight
Claws of Death
Bitter Air
Honey Hunt

Blade On A Train

<u>Fantasy Short Stories:</u>

City of Snow

City of Light

City of Vengeance

Dragons, Goats and Kingdom

Smog The Pathetic Dragon

Don't Go In The Shed

The Tomato Saver

The Remarkable Way She Died

The Bloodied Rose

Asmodia's Wrath

Heart of A Killer

Emissary of Blood

Dragon Coins

Dragon Tea

Dragon Rider

Sacrifice of the Soul

Heart of The Flesheater

Heart of The Regent

Heart of The Standing

Feline of The Lost

Heart of The Story

City of Fire

Awaiting Death

www.ingramcontent.com/pod-product-compliance
Lightning Source LLC
LaVergne TN
LVHW011844060526
838200LV00054B/4154